James Harvey Robinson

TEACHER OF HISTORY

Portrait by Bachrach

James Harvey Robinson
TEACHER OF HISTORY

Luther V. Hendricks

King's Crown Press
Morningside Heights, New York
1946

Copyright 1946 by

LUTHER V. HENDRICKS

Printed in the United States of America

by The Vermont Printing Co., Brattleboro, Vermont

KING'S CROWN PRESS
is a division of Columbia University Press organized for the purpose of making certain scholarly material available at minimum cost. Toward that end, the publishers have adopted every reasonable economy except such as would interfere with a legible format. The work is presented substantially as submitted by the author, without the usual editorial attention of Columbia University Press.

Acknowledgements

GRATEFUL acknowledgments are hereby made to Professor Moses J. Aronson for permission to quote from an article by Lynn Thorndike entitled "James Harvey Robinson 1863-1936" appearing in the *Journal of Social Philosophy*, Vol. I, 1936; to the editors *Chicago Schools Journal* for permission to quote from an article by James Harvey Robinson entitled "The Significance of History in Industrial Education," appearing in the *Educational Bi-Monthly*, Vol. IV, 1910; to the editors of *The Nation* for permission to quote from a review of Robinson's an *Introduction to the History of Western Europe* appearing in *The Nation*, LXXXVI, June 18, 1903; to the American Historical Association for permission to quote from *The Study of History in Secondary Schools*, a Report of the Committee of Five of the American Historical Association, 1911; to Henry Holt and Company for permission to quote from the account of James Harvey Robinson written by Harry Elmer Barnes and appearing in the *American Masters of Social Science*, 1927, and from the preface to *A Political History of Western Europe Since 1814* by Charles Seignobos, translated by Charles M. McVane; to the University of California Press for permission to quote from the preface to the *Syllabus of a Course of Eighty-Seven Lectures in Modern History*, 1899, by H. Morse Stephens; to the Houghton Mifflin Company for permission to quote from *Modern and Contemporary World History, 1918* by J. Salwyn Schapiro; and to Ginn and Company for permission to quote from *The Development of Modern Europe* Vol. II, 1907-08, by James Harvey Robinson and Charles A. Beard and from *An Introduction to the History of Western Europe*, 1934, by James Harvey Robinson.

Preface

SINCE 1890 there has been a great change in history taught in American colleges and schools. Historical instruction during the last decade of the nineteenth century was characterized by a great emphasis on the political, military, and constitutional aspects of the past, while little attention was given to man's achievements in other fields of human endeavor. Although in some college and university classes the lecture served as the basis for historical instruction, both colleges and schools relied mainly on the history textbook. The texts concerned themselves almost exclusively with political, military, and dynastic affairs, were crowded with names and dates, emphasized extraordinary and picturesque events and crises in human affairs, and for the schools at least, often lacked scholarship. Moreover, the reliance of the history teacher upon the material appearing in the text and the practice of using this as a basis for class recitation and questioning gave little opportunity for the student to become acquainted with historical sources or to familiarize himself with the historical method, though some volumes of sources selected for class use became available in the latter years of the century.

During the past fifty years the study of history has been broadened to include the social, economic, cultural, and intellectual activities and achievements of man. Increased attention to these aspects of man's past has been accompanied by reduction in the proportion, and in some cases the amount, of political, military, diplomatic, and constitutional history offered in schools and colleges. At the same time there has been a tendency to rely less upon a single text and to provide students with the opportunity for wider reading and for examining, criticizing, organizing, and interpreting historical sources. Equally significant has been the demand in recent years that history in cooperation with the allied social sciences attempt to explain the present and provide background for understanding contemporary problems. This shift in the aims and emphases of historical instruction has been accompanied by a change in the courses offered at both the collegiate and secondary levels.

In high schools English and medieval history as separate courses have all but disappeared, while ancient history as an independent subject has also come in for decreasing attention. Separate courses in ancient, medieval, modern, and English history have been merged into general survey courses in world history or the history of civilization, extending over a period of one or two years, in which increasing emphasis has been placed upon the modern and contemporary times.

The shift in historical instruction at the college level has revealed the same tendency: less emphasis on ancient, medieval[1] and English history; more attention to the modern and recent periods of history, the development of survey courses in world history and in contemporary civilization,[2] the latter, frequently utilizing subject matter from the several allied social sciences.

These changes, associated with the term "the new history," amount to a revolution in the aims, organization, and content of historical instruction. They were brought about through the activities of educational leaders and various professional associations concerned with bettering historical instruction, through influential reports and recommendations of a series of professional committees interested in improving historical study and of adapting it to the educational requirements of the modern age, and through innovations appearing in textbooks. The one figure prominent in all these agencies of change is James Harvey Robinson.

The purpose of this study is to determine the part played by Robinson in bringing about the twentieth century shift in the aims, content, and organization of the history offered in the colleges and secondary schools. This study does not trace the origins and history of the ideas that constituted Robinson's "new history" (Robinson himself traced some of its antecedents back to Herodotus). The concepts of the "new history" were not, in the main, original with him nor held by him alone. But it was he who most effectively advanced and promoted the "new history" among educators and textbook writers until in effect, he was the "new history." Neither is this an investigation of the contributions of Robinson to higher education, adult education, or to the popularizing of what he called the new knowledge. These are dealt with only incidentally for the purpose of explaining the influences that molded Robinson and to give some indication of the great influence of his ideas, addresses, and

---

1. Joseph R. Strayer, "What is Medieval History?" *Social Education*, vol. IX, November, 1945, p. 293.

2. Sidney R. Packard, "The Introductory College Course in History," *Social Education*, vol. IV, December, 1940, pp. 538-544.

writings on the teaching of history resulting from his prestige as an historian and his recognition as one of the intellectual and educational leaders of his generation. This is a study of Robinson as an educator; another study is needed of Robinson's place in American historiography and in the philosophy of history.

No intensive study has been made of Robinson and his varied career. However there is a brief biographical account of Robinson in Howard W. Odum's *American Masters of Social Science*. This consists of an 87-page chapter prepared by Harry Elmer Barnes, a former student and later associate of Robinson. Barnes' biographical sketch is concerned with the general sweep of Robinson's career as an historian, a college and university teacher, and as a social reformer. It makes no effort to deal with other aspects of Robinson's career as an educator, such as his campaign against the outmoded practices of historical instruction carried on through his numerous articles in professional periodicals and his frequent addresses before the leading professional organizations, the evolution of his concepts of the "new history," his activities in various professional committees concerned with the place of history in the schools, and the influence of Robinson's textbooks upon historical instruction in the colleges and in the secondary schools.

The Robinson papers are in the possession of Clifton H. Bushnell, Robinson's nephew and one time secretary.[3] The collection includes no correspondence for the early period of Robinson's career, though some may exist in the files of those to whom Robinson wrote. Dr. Charles A. Beard, one close associate, indicates however that his letters from Robinson have been destroyed. The most valuable correspondence was a series of weekly letters that Robinson had written to his sister, Sarah, which frequently gave interesting insights into Robinson's ideas and plans. They, for example, show the reason for Robinson's resignation from Columbia, his plans for the New School for Social Research, and some of his ideas on economic and social problems.

The most valuable source for this investigation has been the addresses and writings of Robinson himself, scattered through professional periodicals, and the proceedings, minutes and annual reports of various professional organizations.[4] Equally important were three other major sources, the *New History,* the college and secondary school texts of

---

3. See bibliography, p. 113.
4. See bibliography, p. 113.

which Robinson was author or co-author, and the official reports of professional committees concerned with the place of history in the schools.[5] Unfortunately there exist no notes or records of deliberations of these committees.

Valuable assistance has come also from several of the former students and associates of Robinson who have been most helpful in supplying individual items of information. Those who have been most generous with their time are: Henry Johnson, professor emeritus of history in Teachers College; Harry J. Carman, now dean of Columbia College; Virginia Gildersleeve, dean of Barnard College; James T. Shotwell, Bryce Professor Emeritus of International Relations and director of the Division of Economics and History, the Carnegie Endowment for International Peace; J. Salwyn Schapiro, professor of history in the College of the City of New York; Thomas Jesse Jones, director of the Phelps Stokes Foundation; Alvin Johnson, former president of the New School for Social Research; and Wesley Mitchell, professor emeritus of economics in Columbia and former associate of Robinson at the New School for Social Research.

Special acknowledgment is due to Clifton H. Bushnell and to his sister Mrs. Ruth Van Tuyl for their hospitality, interest, and helpfulness. Mr. Bushnell made every effort to supply me with information concerning Robinson and was most helpful in giving me an intimate picture of Robinson as a man.

Also I should like to acknowledge the assistance of Miss Ruth Seward who read parts of this manuscript from time to time and offered many helpful suggestions.

No words can express adequately my appreciation for the large and generous assistance of Professor Erling M. Hunt of Teachers College, Columbia University, who has given me unsparingly of both his counsel and his time. Without his encouragement and helpful criticism this study would never have been completed.

My acknowledgments would not be complete without a tribute to the encouragement, patience, and assistance of my wife, Emily Shern Hendricks, and my mother, Millie C. Hendricks; the former not only typed all this study from long hand manuscript but also accepted cheerfully the inconveniences of "widowhood."

L. V. H.

5. See bibliography, pp. 114, 116-118.

Table of Contents

I. JAMES HARVEY ROBINSON: HISTORIAN, SCHOLAR AND TEACHER

Early Life	1
Career at the University of Pennsylvania	4
Career at Columbia University	10
Champion of the "New History"	19
A New Adventure in Higher Education	23
Popularizing the New Knowledge	25

II. THE NEW HISTORY

Reaction Against Outmoded Practices of Historical Instruction	29
Aims and Values of the "New History"	32
"New History" and the Historical Method	39
"New History" Emphasizing the Permanent Achievements of Man	40
"New History" and Its Social Science Allies	45
Promoting the "New History" through Addresses and Writings	47
Promoting the "New History" through Membership in Professional Committees	52

III. ROBINSON'S TEXTBOOKS

Publication of Source Material	65
Early College Textbooks	67
Revision of College Textbooks	85
Secondary School Textbooks	89

IV. ROBINSON'S INFLUENCES

    Influence on the Teaching of College History   101

    Influence on the Teaching of Secondary School History   106

V. BIBLIOGRAPHY   113

1
Historian, Scholar, Teacher

JAMES HARVEY ROBINSON was primarily a university scholar and teacher in the field of European history. Yet he influenced not only the organization and content of college and university history courses and the concepts of history held by students and other fellow historians, but the content and organization of secondary-school courses in history and social studies as well. Impatient of traditions and what he considered their deadening influence, he challenged the thinking and the teaching of his more academic colleagues, and attempted to focus the experience of the past on present problems and issues. A scholar and university teacher of recognized standing, whose influence clearly helped to broaden the concept of history held by professional historians, his major publications were nevertheless directed to the general college and secondary-school student and to the more thoughtful reading public.

Though part of Robinson's professional training was obtained in Europe, the influences that molded his thinking seem predominantly American. Robinson was born in Bloomington, Illinois, June 29, 1863. He was of the eighth generation in lineal descent from Dr. John Robinson, pastor of the Pilgrim band that sought freedom for their religious views by emigrating from England to Leyden, Holland. Robinson's first American ancestor was a son of Dr. John Robinson, Isaac, who, after the death of his father at Leyden, came with his mother to Plymouth Colony in 1629.[1]

Robinson's father, also named James Harvey, was born near Saratoga, New York. In 1836 he settled in Bloomington, Illinois, where he established a bank and became highly successful as a business man. In 1842 he married Latracia M. Drake, daughter of a Presbyterian minister who had come from Homer, New York, to Bloomington two years before.[2]

---

1. *Bloomington Pantagraph*, undated clipping in the Bushnell collection. This information is given in a column announcing the death of Charles W. Robinson, eldest brother of James Harvey Robinson.

2. An undated and unidentified clipping in the Bushnell collection. The information is also confirmed by Harry Elmer Barnes, a former student and later

Of this union eight children were born. Two of them died in early life. The others were Sarah D., Mary W., Charles W., John D., James Harvey, and Benjamin.[3]

The Robinson family was well to do and possessed a lively interest in intellectual and cultural matters.[4] One of Robinson's older brothers, Charles, who succeeded his father as head of the bank, accumulated a large library throughout his lifetime; often he said that he never bought a book which he did not wish to read.[5] The youngest brother, Benjamin, became a famous botanist and headed the Harvard herbarium.

Robinson himself was rather over-prepared for the common schools and claimed that he attended them with little advantage. After completing the grade school, he attended Bloomington High School[6] and later the Normal School at Normal, Illinois.[7] There, under the influence of Stephen A. Forbes, Robinson eargerly learned to handle microscopes and prepare slides. Soon he and his brother Benjamin became so impressed by the wonders of nature that they spent hours at home exploring with both microscope and telescope. In particular the science of biology early began to fascinate Robinson. This interest was later intensified by his visits with Benjamin, by that time a distinguished Harvard botanist, and by his association with the biologists and embryologists at Columbia.[8] Even in his later years he revealed his interest in science by often taking along on various trips his microscope in order to examine more carefully the minute animal and plant life of field and stream.[9] The knowledge resulting from his own studies and observations enabled him to appreciate the refined methods of the scientists and their concern with the evolution and devolopment of common things. Barnes tells us, and it seems to be substantiated in the *New History*, that Robinson's interest in and knowledge of science made it easier for

associate. See his essay on James Harvey Robinson in Howard W. Odum, *American Masters of Social Science*, New York, Henry Holt, 1927, p. 321.

3. *Ibid.*
4. Barnes, *loc. cit.*, p. 321.
5. *Bloomington Pantagraph*, undated clipping referred to in footnote 1.
6. Barnes, *loc. cit.*, p. 323.
7. Henry Johnson, *The Other Side of Main Street*, New York, Columbia University Press, 1943, p. 156.
8. Barnes, *loc. cit.*, p. 325.
9. Interview with Clifton H. Bushnell, Robinson's nephew, and one-time secretary, December 13, 1944. Also confirmed in interview with Goodwin Watson, January 19, 1945.

him to visualize the evolutionary process present in the development of civilization.[10]

In 1882 Robinson went to Europe and spent a year in what Barnes describes as "rather unintelligent efforts to improve his French and his flute playing."[11] On his return to Bloomington he worked for a few months as a clerk in a local store and later accepted a position in the family bank. Finally, in 1884, he decided to enter Harvard, at the same time that his well-prepared young brother Benjamin was entering as a sophomore. Robinson completed the four-year course in three years and remained for an additional year to earn his master of arts degree in 1888. Just before starting his fourth year at Harvard, he married Grace Read, daughter of Mr. and Mrs. Charles E. Read of Bloomington. Mr. Read was a prominent and successful hardware merchant in Bloomington for many years.[12]

Robinson, according to Barnes, expressed the conviction that William James was the only teacher who left a significant and permanent impression on him or in anyway influenced his later thinking. James was given the credit for not only encouraging a pluralistic and pragmatic philosophy and a critical view of knowledge but also for arousing in Robinson the interest in psychology which became influential in Robinson's later thinking.[13]

In 1888 Robinson again went to Europe, this time to spend a semester studying German at Strasbourg, where his brother Benjamin was studying botany. After one semester at Strasbourg he moved to the University of Freiburg, where he received careful training in the technique and methodology of historical research. While continuing his graduate study, he had the opportunity to work with a vast amount of source material. This training and experience in Germany are largely responsible for the remarkable facility for minute and painstaking research which was evidenced early in his career as an historian.

At Freiburg he had been welcomed by Von Holst, who encouraged Robinson to rework the paper which he had done at Harvard on "The Original and Derived Features of the Constitution of the United States

---

10. Barnes, *loc. cit.,* p. 325. J. H. Robinson, *The New History,* New York, Macmillan, 1912, pp. 128-30.
11. Barnes, *loc. cit.,* p. 326.
12. *Bloomington Bulletin,* April 30, 1911.
13. Barnes, *loc. cit.,* pp. 326-7.

of America." This became the subject of his doctor's dissertation. He received his doctor of philosophy degree from Freiburg in 1890.

Thus Robinson completed his formal preparation for scholarship at the age of 27, with no experience as a teacher and with no notable variations from the pattern of preparation rather common to young American historians of his day, except perhaps for an interest in science and psychology and brief business experience.

CAREER AT THE UNIVERSITY OF PENNSYLVANIA

Robinson, on completion of his graduate study at Freiburg, remained for some time in Germany. During a visit in Halle, he met Simon N. Patten, professor of political economy at the University of Pennsylvania.[14] The latter was so impressed with the young historian that he offered him a position as lecturer in history at the University of Pennsylvania.[15] Robinson accepted and, after serving in this capacity during 1891-1892, was promoted to an associate professorship, a position which he held until his resignation in 1895.

At the University of Pennsylvania, Robinson, with his alert and inquiring mind and his excellent training in the methodology of research, found an intellectual atmosphere that was both challenging and stimulating. His immediate associates in the history department were Edward P. Cheyney, whose field was English history, and Dana C. Munro, who specialized in the medieval period, both men progressive members of his guild. The daily contact of these three young men offered much opportunity for an exchange of opinion and mutual stimulation.[16] There also, in the field of American history, John Bach McMaster was writing his volumes on the *History of the People of the United States,* new and interesting histories which were arousing wide attention and speculation as to the newer prospects and possibilities of history portraying the more varied activities of the past, including those of the common man. Since these three, Cheyney, McMaster, and Munro, were all comparatively

---

14. Patten was a leading economist of the time and was instrumental in laying the foundations for the new Wharton School of Business. E. P. Cheyney, *History of the University of Pennsylvania,* Philadelphia, University of Pennsylvania Press, 1940, p. 289.

15. Barnes, *loc. cit.,* p. 328.

16. *Ibid.,* In a letter to Barnes Dr. Cheyney tells how they worked together enthusiastically. Further evidence of their cooperation is their famous series of *Translations and Reprints from the Original Sources of European History.*

recent appointees to the University of Pennsylvania, the department was little bound by tradition or conservatism but rather was one in which an alert newcomer would find encouragement to experiment and set new patterns.

Equal stimulation was present outside of the history department as well, especially in the department of Political Economy, headed by Simon N. Patten, who had become a close friend of Robinson since their acquaintance in Europe. Professor Patten's challenging ideas and varied activities were the center of many wholesome economic and social disputes both within and outside the university.[17] His interest and speculation in the history of thought and institutions are credited with exerting considerable influence on Robinson's early career.[18] Probably equally significant was Robinson's acquaintance with E. G. Conklin, who became one of the leaders in the effort to indicate the historical and cultural implications of modern biology and genetics.[19]

Cheyney observed that in a short time the intellectual atmosphere of the University was extended beyond the academic confines by Robinson himself, who, soon after arriving at Philadelphia, had begun to associate with many of the intellectual leaders of the city.[20] Henry C. Lea undoubtedly stimulated greatly Robinson's interest in sources, in the Middle Ages, and in the medieval church.

Harry Elmer Barnes, has suggested that the custom of associating with intellectual leaders outside his field and often with those entirely removed from academic life did much to prevent Robinson from being an esoteric and monastic scholar. Furthermore these contacts served to stimulate the humanistic tendencies and broaden the vision of the young historian.[21]

Robinson's career as a professor of history began in an especially propitious time, a time when historical scholarship was just coming into its own in America. The teaching and writing of history during the first half of the nineteenth century had been largely left to men of letters,

---

17. Cheyney, *op. cit.*, pp. 289-294.
18. Barnes, *loc. cit.*, p. 329.
19. *Ibid.*
20. *Ibid.*, pp. 329-30. This statement appears in a letter from Cheyney to Barnes. There is much evidence to the fact that he kept this practice up throughout the remainder of his life. His weekly letters to his sister Sarah are filled with comments on these gatherings (Bushnell Collection).
21. Barnes, *loc. cit.*, p. 329.

clergymen, or teachers in other fields who devoted their spare time to the study and writing of history. In the colleges and universities it fared poorly. Very often it received only the benevolent attention of some professor who had already given his best energy to his own special field of endeavor.

However from 1870 to the end of the century the teaching and writing of history underwent a great transformation. It became truly professionalized. This great change is revealed by the establishment of many special graduate schools for the training of students in historical scholarship. Some of these were: the School of Political Science which later became the College of History and Political Science at Cornell University; the Graduate Faculty of Political Science at Columbia, and the School of Political Science at the University of Michigan. Equally significant were the famous seminars in history being offered in Johns Hopkins University, out of which grew one of the most influential enterprises of American historical scholarship, the *Johns Hopkins University Studies in Historical and Political Sciences*.[22] Further manifestation of the professionalization of the study and teaching of history came with the establishment of the American Historical Association in 1884, a national organization dedicated to the promotion of historical scholarship in America.

Thus, by the time Robinson began to offer his first courses at the University of Pennsylvania, the teaching and writing of history had truly become a profession. In spite of its great progress, however, the full potentialities of history had by no means been explored, and many new challenges and opportunities were open to all those interested in a career of historical scholarship.

Robinson's undergraduate courses at the University of Pennsylvania were concerned with three general areas of European history: the Renaissance and Reformation, the French Revolution and Napoleonic era, and European history since 1815.[23] In addition he offered two graduate courses: the Antecedents of the Reformation, and the Early Years of the French Revolution. These, a combination of lecture and seminar

---

22. Herbert Baxter Adams, *The Study of History in American Colleges and Universities,* Bureau of Education Circular of Information No. 2, 1887, pp. 134, 75, 115, 197.
23. University of Pennsylvania, *Catalogue of Announcements* 1893-94, pp. 62-63.

TEACHER OF HISTORY

courses,[24] proved to be not just another series of graduate courses in history; from the very beginning of his career his foremost aim was to make his courses vital and interesting. His alert mind made possible a penetrating interpretation of historical material and consequently aroused the interest and enthusiasm of his students.[25]

Cheyney, his colleague, said that Robinson was fundamentally a teacher, intent on effectively presenting his material to his classes. One of his methods was to write on the blackboard an outline of his lecture before beginning his talk. Such a procedure impressed the students as indicative that he knew exactly the scope of his lecture and what points he wished to clarify.[26] Cheyney further observed that the most significant fact of Robinson's whole career was that he was fundamentally a well-trained, solid, historical student with a rigorous conception of historical research and statement.[27]

His teaching at the University of Pennsylvania exemplified the highest traditions, aims, and methods of the historian of the latter part of the nineteenth century: namely, a painstaking and minute search for facts gleaned directly from the original sources used in the setting of their own time to reconstruct the past.[28] This process, as many of his students testified, became a pleasant experience when tempered by his keen mind, his facility for developing illuminating and contemporary illustrations, and his genuine interest in teaching.

One of the first indications of Robinson's expanding interest in the teaching of history was revealed when he accepted membership on the sub-committee on History, Civil Government and Political Economy of the Committee on Secondary School Studies of the National Education Association. This sub-committee, which met in Madison, Wisconsin, in 1892, marked the first attempt on the part of any national organization to make a survey of the teaching of history in the secondary schools. In

24. *Ibid.*, 1894-5, pp. 167, 176.
25. Barnes, *loc. cit.*, p. 376.
26. Barnes, *loc. cit.*, pp. 377-378. Letter from Cheyney to Barnes.
27. *Ibid.*, pp. 334-5. An understanding of this basic element in Robinson's makeup is most essential if we are to understand his full career.
28. Nineteenth century history came to be characterized by Leopold von Ranke, who, in 1824 in his *Geschichte der romanischen und germanischen Völker,* disclaimed any intention of judging the past or of using it for the instruction of the present but stated that he merely wanted to show *wie es eigentlich gewesen.*

accepting this appointment Robinson had his first opportunity to view the teaching of history on the secondary level.

Early in his career at the University of Pennsylvania Robinson revealed another interest, that of editing and writing. In 1891 he revised and published in English his work on the German Bundesrath,[29] and in the following year he became assistant editor of the *Annals* of the American Academy of Political and Social Science, a position which he held until he left the University of Pennsylvania in 1895.[30] His interest in German constitutional history and his desire to make the sources more easily available for American students led him, in 1894, to translate and edit *The Constitution of the Kingdom of Prussia*. This translation was accompanied by an introduction and many explanatory footnotes.[31] In the same year Robinson and his colleagues Cheyney and Munro initiated their famous series of *Translations and Reprints from the Original Sources of European History*. Robinson was responsible for six of this series: "The French Revolution, 1789-1791," "The Napoleonic Period," "The Period of Early Reformation in Germany," "The Restoration of the European Policy of Metternich 1814-1820," "The Pre-Reformation Period," and "Protest of the Cour des Aides of Paris, 10 April, 1775."[32]

Something of the care and effort that Robinson put into this project may be gathered from Munro, one of his colleagues in the enterprise: "He did the work so thoroughly and conscientiously that, as he had said, it would have been easier to write a volume on the subject than to prepare one of these numbers."[33]

In addition to his early works as editor and translator while at the University of Pensylvania two articles were published by Robinson. Both indicate that he developed early some of the ideas about history that he long maintained. The first article contained a discussion of

---

29. Robinson, *The German Bundesrath, A Study on Comparative Constitutional Law,* Philadelphia, 1891, pp. 68; (Publications of the University of Pennsylvania. Political Economic and Public Law Series, III).

30. American Academy of Political and Social Science, *Annals,* 1892-5.

31. Robinson, "The Constitution of the Kingdom of Prussia," American Academy of Political and Social Science, *Annals,* 1894, Part 2 supplement to volume V.

32. *Translations and Reprints frrom the Original Sources of European History* I-V Department of History of the University of Pennsylvania, 1894-7.

33. Barnes, *loc. cit.,* p. 335. Letter from Munro to Barnes, February 25, 1926.

Henry Sidgwick's *Elements of Politics*,[34] and the other concerned what he believed to be the excessive emphasis placed upon the Tennis Court Oath in considering the French Revolution.[35] In the introduction to his discussion of Sidgwick's *Elements of Politics,* he acknowledged the historian's debt to the political scientists and the sociologists in helping to explain many activities and interests of man in the past. He suggested further that the historian would find that much of the information supplied by these allied social scientists would prove to be most helpful in the future. In speaking of the potential influence of sociology on the study of history, he said: "Sociology . . . although just getting on its feet, not content with modifying our ideas of the present, may well introduce a corresponding radical alteration in our manner of viewing the past; in particular the long recognized method of treating historical events."[36] This would indicate that Robinson, as an historian, early recognized the influence of the newer allied social sciences on the study of man and man's past, and was quite eager to have the historian utilize their findings for his own purposes.

His second article, entitled "The Tennis Court Oath," was inspired by his belief that his fellow historians and writers of history textbooks were all too often giving exaggerated attention to the dramatic events in history. He felt that a notable example of this was the extended attention frequently given the Tennis Court Oath in the study of the French Revolution and events leading directly to it. In describing the Tennis Court Oath Robinson attempted to show that there was no sudden, unexpected move; as a result of a succession of events, and judging from the attitude expressed by the leading minds from time to time, it was inevitable. Therefore it was not historically valid to dwell upon the Tennis Court Oath as an isolated incident, as historians had frequently done; in so doing they were giving the wrong historical perspective and ignoring the basic law of historical continuity.[37]

34. Robinson, "Sidgwick's Elements of Politics," *Annals of the American Academy of Political and Social Science,* September 1892, vol. III, pp. 211-222. (Henry Sidgwick, *Elements of Politics,* London, Macmillan, 1891.)
35. Robinson, "The Tennis Court Oath," *Annual Report of the American Historical Association,* 1894, pp. 541-547.
36. Robinson, "Sidgwick's Elements of Politics," *Annals of the American Academy of Political and Social Science,* 1892, vol. III, p. 211.
37. Robinson, "The Tennis Court Oath," *Annual Report of the American Historical Association,* 1894, pp. 541-547.

While at the University of Pennsylvania Robinson established his interest in European history (particularly in the Reformation and French Revolution); his belief in the necessity for both the student and historian to examine the original sources in order to obtain the most accurate and real understanding of the past; his disapproval of the type of history that overemphasizes the dramatic episodes and thus ignored the law of historical continuity; his recognition of the importance to the historian of the allies of history, especially, political science and sociology; and lastly his ability as an editor through his work on the *Translations and Reprints* and the *Annals*. At the same time his continued interest in science was demonstrated by his association with E. G. Conklin. Probably most significant, in the light of his later activities, was his genuine interest in making the teaching of history more effective, an interest evidenced in his classes and through his participation as a member of the subcommittee on History, Civil Government and Political Economy of the Committee on Secondary School Studies of the National Education Association, meeting in 1892.

CAREER AT COLUMBIA UNIVERSITY

Robinson, after his four years on the faculty of the University of Pennsylvania, went to Columbia University in 1895 as professor of European history. Technically his appointment was in Barnard College, and his salary and professorship were based on the Barnard Foundation. Through an agreement in effect at this time between Columbia and Barnard College, Barnard was to pay the salaries of two professors to be added to the Faculty of Political Science but whose services would be rendered partly at Columbia, "provided that for every hour given by them to Columbia, a member of the existing staff should give an hour to Barnard."[38] Thus from the beginning Robinson divided his time between Barnard and Columbia. (He was, incidentally, acting Dean of Barnard for the school year of 1900-01.)

Robinson's invitation to Columbia was part of a general movement to strengthen the Faculty of Political Science by adding a specialist in medieval and modern history. To this time at Columbia there had been no professor or associate who had specialized in European history. The

---

38. Alice D. Muller, *Barnard College, the First Fifty Years*, Columbia University Press, 1939, p. 54.

few general courses covering this area were taught by William Dunning, Herbert L. Osgood, or a lecturer.[39] Barnes believes that Professor Dunning had suggested Robinson because of the latter's reputation as a student familiar with original source material and because of his demonstrated skill as an editor.[40]

Robinson remained for nearly a quarter of a century at Columbia, firmly establishing during these years his standing as an historian. During his early years Robinson continued his interest, developed at the University of Pennsylvania, in translating and editing source material. In addition to contributing to the later numbers of the *Translations and Reprints, from the Original Sources of European History*, he, with the collaboration of Henry W. Rolfe, professor of Latin at Swarthmore, published *Petrarch, The First Modern Scholar and Man of Letters*.[41] This volume contained source material designed to illuminate the beginnings of the Renaissance.

His other historical writings consisted of specialized studies presented in papers before professional organizations and of similar articles written for professional periodicals. These were concerned with two phases of European history, the Medieval Church and the Reformation, and the French Revolution.

Two of his discussions dealing with the church and the Reformation were "Sacred and Profane History,"[42] which he read before the American Historical Association, and "The Study of the Lutheran Revolt," which appeared in the *American Historical Review*.[43] In these discussions Robinson was warning against prejudice, that the real significance of the medieval church as both a religious and political force must be understood to give an understanding of the history of Europe.

Two additional articles were related to the French Revolution: "The Declaration of the Rights of Man"[44] in the *Political Science Quarterly*

---

39. *Columbia College Catalogue*, 1893-95.
40. Barnes, *loc. cit.*, p. 337.
41. James H. Robinson and Henry W. Rolfe, *Petrarch, The First Modern Scholar and Man of Letters*, New York, Putnam, 1898.
42. Robinson, "Sacred and Profane History," *Annual Report of the American Historical Association*, 1899, vol. I, pp. 529-535.
43. Robinson, "The Study of the Lutheran Revolt," *American Historical Review*, VIII, 1903, pp. 205-216.
44. Robinson, "The Declaration of the Rights of Man," *Political Science Quarterly*, vol. XIV, 1906, pp. 653-62.

and "Recent Tendencies in the Study of the French Revolution"[45] in the *American Historical Review*.

In several of his articles Robinson pointed out the error of over-emphasizing dramatic episodes, such as Luther's burning of the canon law and the Declaration of the Rights of Man. By stressing such episodes, the historians, he warned again, were really ignoring the law of historical continuity and consequently were failing to place events in their proper historical perspective. Robinson had for some time deplored this tendency on the part of historians, for about ten years earlier he had made the same criticism of the treatment of the Tennis Court Oath by writers of histories.[46]

These articles published during his early years at Columbia reveal Robinson's continued interest in the areas of the Reformation and the French Revolution and, above all, his desire to see the historian obtain the most accurate picture of what actually happened. In spite of the fact that these interests seemed to be uppermost during his early career, his activities as a classroom teacher soon began to reflect a broadening interest in history and its educational possibilities.

At Columbia University Robinson's impressionable mind received stimulus and inspiration from many sources. The successive ideas and personalities with which Robinson came into contact are reflected in his changing interests as an historian and educator. His early associates in the Faculty of Political Science at Columbia numbered some of the most distinguished scholars in America. Included were Dean John W. Burgess, who in 1880 had organized the Faculty of Political Science, Herbert L. Osgood who was beginning his monumental history on the American Colonies: William A. Dunning, who was preparing his essays on Reconstruction: and William M. Sloan, an authority in modern European history.[47] Further stimulation was offered by other educators and scholars who came to Columbia after the turn of the century. One of the most important of these was Charles A. Beard who shortly after arriving at Columbia in 1903 formed a close friendship with Robinson that lasted until the latter's death. Although it is difficult to measure the

45. Robinson, "Recent Tendencies in the Study of the French Revolution," *American Historical Review*, vol. XI, pp. 529-47.
46. Robinson, "The Tennis Court Oath," *Annual Report of the American History Association*, 1894, pp. 541-547.
47. Professor Sloan came to Columbia in 1896, one year after the arrival of Robinson.

influence of the alert and original Beard it does appear that he was responsible for Robinson's increased attention to economic history and perhaps helped to overcome some of Robinson's lack of interest in English history.

Others at Columbia who undoubtedly influenced Robinson were professors John Dewey and Henry Johnson of Teachers College. Dewey's demand that education be made functional was clearly in accord with views stated in Robinson's "new history." It would also appear that Johnson, one of the most prominent authorities on the teaching of history, furnished further stimulation to Robinson in their frequent discussions of history and historical instruction.[48]

Further inspiration came to Robinson from another important source; a number of alert and enterprising graduate students who after completing their studies remained, at least temporarily, as assistants or instructors in history at Columbia. Some of these such as William R. Shepherd, James T. Shotwell, Carlton J. H. Hayes and Lynn Thorndike remained at Columbia permanently while others such as Dixon Ryan Fox, Louise Loomis and William K. Boyd later associated themselves with other colleges and universities.

One of the most progressive of Robinson's earlier graduate students was Shepherd who received his doctorate in 1896.[49] After teaching some courses in medieval and modern history, he initiated in 1898, a course entitled the Epochs of Ancient and Medieval Europe which was required of all candidates for the baccalaureate degree. This course by 1901 included a well rounded account of the social, economic cultural and intellectual aspects of the past; the same comprehensive treatment that had been urged by Robinson for nearly a decade.[50]

Thus it is evident that during Robinson's years at Columbia he had the good fortune of being in frequent contact with many of the most scholarly and progressive leaders in American intellectual life.

During his first eight years at Columbia, Robinson offered a wide range of courses. They appeared in the Columbia College Catalogues as follows: The Middle Ages and the Renaissance, Sixteenth Century to

48. Henry Johnson, *The Other Side of Main Street*, p. 161. Also interview with Johnson, June 3, 1945.
49. Barnes, *loc. cit.*, p. 379. Shepherd in a letter to Barnes describes his impression of Robinson as a teacher.
50. William R. Shepherd, *A Syllabus of the Epochs of History*, New York, Columbia University in the City of New York, 1901.

the Peace of Augsburg, Political History of Europe from the Peace of Augsburg to the Peace of Westphalia, The Period of Louis XIV and the Antecedents of the French Revolution, Europe and the French Revolution, Europe and Napoleon, The Sources of Medieval and Modern Continental History,[51] Seminar in Modern European History, Opening of the Lutheran Reformation, Medieval Institutions and Culture, Historical Bibliography and the Development of European Culture During the Middle Ages.[52]

During these years, Robinson reorganized his courses in many ways. Sometimes small areas were studied intensively; at other times small areas were combined so as to offer large sweeps of history.[53] Besides his general courses and courses on limited areas of history, he offered, from the begining of his teaching at Columbia, research courses of various types. These were variously designated as seminars, courses in historical method, and bibliographical courses. In some he was the sole instructor; in others, different members of the department worked with him.[54] Something of the caliber of work required for these advanced research courses may be gathered by the fact that students, before entering the class, were required to have a fluent knowledge of French, German, and Latin.[55]

Out of these varied teaching and research activities Robinson began relatively early to manifest an increased interest in the cultural and intellectual aspects of history. This development can best be traced through the changing title of, and shifting emphasis in, his general course in the Middle Ages and the Renaissance. During seven years, the course was listed as follows:[56]

1895-6 The Middle Ages and Renaissance

51. This was a course in the methods of historical study.
52. These were the courses offered by Robinson during his first few years at Columbia College as listed in the *Columbia College Catalogues* from 1895-1903.
53. Sometimes courses on the French Revolution and Napoleon were combined; at other times they were taught separately. *Columbia College Catalogue*, 1895-6, p. 81; 1896-7, p. 88.
54. *Columbia College Catalogue* 1895-6; p. 81; 1896-7, p. 85; 1901-2, p. 117.
55. *Columbia College Catalogue* 1899-1900, p. 109; also *Catalogue* for 1900-1902, p. 117. For some of the informal activities of these classes see p. 00.
56. *Columbia College Catalogue*, 1895-6, p. 81; 1897-9, p. 110; 1899-1900, p. 109; 1900-01, p. 112; 1901-02, p. 117.

1897-8 Introduction to Modern European History: Renaissance and Reformation
1899-1900 Antecedents of Modern European History: The Reformation
1900-1 Development of European Culture during the Middle Ages and Renaissance: The Reformation
1901-2 Development of European Culture during the Later Middle Ages and Renaissance: The Protestant Revolt.

Apparently Robinson did not consider the cultural phase of man's development important enough to mention in course titles until 1900. After this it was consistently mentioned in connection with the general course until 1904. Then his interest in the intellectual phase of European history led him to designate this course as the "Intellectual History of Western Europe."[57]

His courses at Columbia, more varied than those at the University of Pennsylvania, continued to be characterized by high scholarship based upon the careful reconstruction of the past through minute examination of the original sources. Men who had been in Robinson's classes and who had been his associates emphasized this characteristic. Professor James T. Shotwell has said that Robinson demanded of himself and others a strict interpretation of original sources. Never did he allow a careless reference to or a mere restatement of secondary material. A student's imagination was controlled and yet stimulated by working with the sources.[58] The late Alexander C. Flick, another of Robinson's earlier students, recalled that Robinson often asked a few students to his home where he read from historical sources sometimes in the original language, sometimes in translation.[59]

---

57. In 1904-5 he omitted the word *culture* and called his course the "Intellectual History of Western Europe from the Breakup of the Roman Empire to the Protestant Revolt." This course in "Intellectual History" became his famous course at Columbia. Of course it was modified as to content and presentation from time to time. Also, at this point Robinson chose to use the term *Protestant Revolt* as being more appropriate and meaningful in labeling the reactions against the Catholic Church than the term *Reformation*, which was widely used.

58. This is contained in a letter from James T. Shotwell to Barnes dated April 15, 1926, and refers to Robinson's class at Columbia in 1895 or 1896. Barnes, *loc. cit.*, p. 349. President Seth Low in his annual report for 1896 stated that Robinson's classes were well attended and much appreciated, Columbia University in the City of New York, *Seventh Annual Report*, p. 39.

59. Barnes, *loc. cit.*, pp. 383-4.

Vivid sidelights on Robinson's conduct of a class were recorded by two of his students. Flick described classroom procedure of Robinson's first two years at Columbia:

> He enjoyed bringing an armful of books into the classroom which, after a brief description of their value, were passed around the class.
> From cards about the size of a postcard, which he took out of his right hand pocket, he lectured to the class. His diction was slow, but his points were remarkably well-organized, and his wit was subtle. He seldom asked questions of his class but encouraged questions from the class. I never saw a teacher who more frankly admitted his ignorance on unfamiliar points. He never posed and never bluffed. He seemed to enjoy smashing smug convictions and emphatic opinions. There was something stimulating in contact with him.[60]

Professor Henry Johnson wrote that Robinson seldom gave a formal lecture in graduate courses but first suggested collateral readings and then spent the rest of the class time in a critical and original discussion and interpretation of the source material which had been previously assigned. Also Robinson often warned against dogmatism, usually quoting from Abelard's *Sic et non*, "By doubting we learn to inquire; by inquiry we find out truth."[61]

As has been previously indicated, Robinson offered, in 1904, his first class in intellectual history, The Intellectual History of Western Europe. This course originally covered the period from the breakup of the Roman Empire to the Protestant Revolt,[62] but in 1908 was expanded to include the intellectual history of Europe from the Augustan period to the eighteenth century.[63] In 1909 the boundaries of this course were again extended to include thought from the Greek Sophists to the French Philosophers. The following year the class was designated as the History of the Intellectual Class of Europe from the Greek Sophists to the French Philosophers. This title with some modifications as to scope was continued throughout Robinson's stay in Columbia and later under David Muzzey and Lynn Thorndike.[64]

Robinson gave more and more attention to this course, and its popu-

---

60. *Ibid.*
61. Henry Johnson, *The Other Side of Main Street*, p. 162.
62. *Columbia College Catalogue*, 1904-5, p. 119.
63. *Ibid.*, 1908-09, p. 92; 1907-08, p. 96.
64. *Ibid.*, 1909-10, p. 109; also see subsequent catalogues.

larity became so great that it was split into three sections.⁶⁵ In the academic year 1914-1915, he offered for the first time a companion course on the advanced graduate level, designated as an Advanced Course in the Intellectual History of Europe during the Greek, Roman and Medieval Period.⁶⁶ These two courses in intellectual history became his only offering from 1916 until his retirement from Columbia in 1919.⁶⁷

His general course, the "History of the Intellectual Class of Europe," became one of the most famous academic enterprises of its time.⁶⁸ It was the result of a gradual development rather than a conscious and abrupt product of any definite period of his teaching career.⁶⁹ Barnes noted that it had its beginnings shortly after Robinson's call to Columbia, when he required a small group of students to read selected sources in the intellectual history of the particular period under consideration. Later he combined the intellectual history of the periods which he had presented in his major courses: namely, the history of the intellectual life of the Middle Ages, the pre-Reformation period, and eighteenth-century France. The resulting course departed more and more from a reading of, and commentary upon, the source material, and gradually took on the characteristics of an interpretation of the salient personalities and types of thought of each age.⁷⁰ This course, which had first concerned itself with the history of the intellectual life of the Middle Ages, pre-Reformation period, and eighteenth-century France, was gradually extended in scope. From his early interest in the intellectual life of the Middle Ages he worked back in reverse chronological order, through the pagan and oriental cultures to a study of the mind of primitive man and even to animal behavior. Likewise his interest in science led him forward from the French Revolution to the phenomenal growth of modern science and its effects upon material culture and the world of ideas. Thus as Robinson's course developed it became more universal in scope and interpretative in character.⁷¹

65. *Ibid.*, 1914-15, p. 138. Carlton J. H. Hayes describes the course as exclusively medieval until about 1912-13 when some modern history was incorporated in it.
66. *Ibid.*, p. 138.
67. *Ibid.*, 1914-15 to 1918-1919.
68. Irwin Edman, *Philosopher's Holiday*, New York, Viking Press, 1938, pp. 134-136.
69. Barnes, *loc. cit.*, p. 375.
70. *Ibid.*, p. 375.
71. *Ibid.*, p. 375.

Although he already was distinctly successful as teacher, the change in his historical interests as manifested in his courses inevitably resulted in an ever-increasing popularity of his courses. During this last year at Columbia his classes were so large that it was necessary to resort to the chemistry laboratory in Havemeyer Hall in order to accommodate all the students in this now famous class in Intellectual History.[72] Reasons for its great popularity may be gathered from students who have preserved for us Robinson's classroom manner in their accounts of their experiences in his classes. One of these later students in Robinson's career at Columbia recalled how Robinson's "eyes would twinkle as he threw an intellectual bomb at us, and tilting back in his chair, would watch the repercussions."[73] Another of his later students, Barnes, pictured Robinson's dry manner, drawling tones, impassivity—although after a brilliant witticism he might pause to observe the effect on the class members and then laugh with them.[74]

Barnes, along with others, analyzed the elements of Robinson's success in holding the interest of even his largest classes. He made up his lectures as he went along but was capable of seizing upon the most important facts and generalizations related to the lecture topic; he never wandered into irrelevancies but kept a clear path before the students. He held a class intent by his sheer intellectual ability, never by rhetoric or dramatics. He had command of subtle but penetrating irony and satire. His success was an "outstanding example of what may be achieved in the way of pedagogical success through turning loose a profound but playful mind upon vital historical materials."[75] Irwin Edman wrote that Robinson enjoyed examining the origins of human stupidity and showing the primitive and immature sides of our minds. The undergraduates "enjoyed the sallies, the freshness, the irreverence, and enjoyed too the fundamental feeling that lay at the basis of it all . . . that man if he took his own intelligence into his own hands could make the world less a shambles and idiocy that it had so often been."[76]

72. *Ibid.*, p. 339.
73. Letter to the writer, March 27, 1945, from Miss Meme J. Heacock, former student of Robinson and now a librarian at Teachers College, Columbia University. In his earlier years Robinson customarily stood during his classes.
74. Barnes, *loc. cit.*, pp. 384-6.
75. *Ibid.*
76. Edman, *Philosopher's Holiday*, pp. 135-6.

Thus Robinson was able to influence some thousands of students who attended Columbia during the first and second decades of the present century.[77] Unfortunately we can neither turn back the clock and sit in Robinson's famous class nor can we turn to a manual and read in detail the brilliant interpretation of the past which he gave to his students. However, the general philosophy of this celebrated course was embodied in *The Mind in the Making*,[78] which he published in 1921. This volume is not a history dealing with the main events of the past in the usual sense but is more an investigation into the origins of our contemporary intelligence, an investigation of those elements, historical and psychological, which have gone into the making of our modern mind. Robinson assumed the role of social reformer[79] as well as interpreter of the past, and entered an eloquent plea for an educational and social milieu which would produce minds fit and free to solve the problems of the present day.[80] The complete skeptic of early years was gradually transformed into a missionary.

CHAMPION OF THE NEW HISTORY

Very early in his career Robinson had revealed an earnest desire to make the study of history contribute more effectively to the educational requirements of our modern age. The first intimation of his concern with this problem, as has been indicated, occurred as early as 1892 when he was serving as a member of the sub-committee on History, Civil Government, and Political Economy of the Committee on Secondary School Studies of the National Education Association.[81] Thenceforth for the next two decades Robinson gave increasing attention to the problem of bringing the study of history into line with the newer discoveries concerning man's past and with the educational needs of our own age. During these twenty years he criticized the aims, methods, and content of the traditional type of history courses then being offered and suggested numerous ways in which the shortcomings could be overcome.

---

77. Barnes, *loc. cit.*, p. 339.
78. Robinson, *The Mind in the Making,* New York, Harper, 1921.
79. This interest became quite marked in his last chapter entitled "The Spirit of Conservatism the Light of History" appearing in his *New History. The Mind in the Making* really represents the flowering of this interest.
80. *The Nation,* January 18, 1922, p. 75.
81. National Education Association *Report of the Committee on Secondary School Studies,* Washington, Government Printing Office, 1893.

Robinson's campaign for improving the teaching of history was reinforced by his activities in many professional organizations, such as the American Historical Association, the Association of Colleges and Preparatory Schools of the Middle States and Maryland, the Herbart Society, the New England History Teachers' Association, the Association of History Teachers of the Middle States and Maryland, and the National Education Association.[82] In 1912 he brought together his ideas on the nature and methods of history in a volume entitled *The New History*.[83]

The progress of his thinking from the Von Ranke conception that the function of history was to discover just what actually occurred was demonstrated by the chief ideas which he expressed in *The New History*. They embraced several definite conceptions and aspirations; namely: (1) history in explaining how things came about was to embrace the law of historical continuity; (2) it was to be comprehensive in content, concerning itself with everything that man had ever done or thought since he first appeared on earth; (3) it was to welcome the aid of the other social sciences such as psychology, sociology, and anthropology; (4) its primary interest was to be in interpreting historical data with special emphasis on the more recent period of history; (5) historical knowledge should be selected, organized, and applied in the interest of social betterment.[84]

Robinson attempted to apply and spread his ideas not only by carrying on a campaign for a new as well as a revitalized history through his professional contacts with historians and educators but also by publishing a series of history texts. In 1902-3 he published a two-volume college text on European history, *An Introduction to the History of Western Europe*.[85] This was so well received that in 1907-8 with the collaboration of his colleague, Charles A. Beard, he published another called

82. American Historical Association, *Annual Report*, 1896, vol. I, pp. 267-278. Association of Colleges and Preparatory Schools of the Middle States and Maryland, *Proceedings* 1894, pp. 38-44 and *Proceedings* for 1898, pp. 8-12. *Fifth Yearbook of the National Herbart Society*, 1899, pp. 42-68. New England History Teachers' Association, *Report of the Spring Meeting* 1906, pp. 1-27, Association of History Teachers of the Middle States and Maryland, *Minutes of the Second Annual Meeting*, II, 1904, 30-38. *Educational Bi-Monthly*, vol. IV, 1910, 376-389.
83. Robinson, *The New History*, New York, Macmillan, 1912.
84. *Ibid*.
85. Robinson, *An Introduction to the History of Western Europe*, 2 vols., Boston, Ginn. 1902-3. Later edition appeared in 1924 and 1934.

the *Development of Modern Europe*.⁸⁶ These college texts were followed by a series of high school texts that were widely used.⁸⁷

While Robinson's interest in making history contribute its share to the educational needs of students occupied a considerable amount of his attention and undoubtedly influenced his later views on the aims and purposes of history, there were other factors contributing to his new viewpoint. Barnes tells us that Robinson through his study of history especially the antecedents of the French Revolution and the Reformation, had become interested in the genesis of institutions and even of civilization as a whole. Thus he was led to give more attention to the middle ages, ancient history and to *Pithecanthropus Erectus*. This procedure, which Barnes called the genetic approach, was further stimulated by Robinson's contacts with the Rationalists, especially Voltaire, who became Robinson's hero.⁸⁸

Barnes acknowledged that Robinson had read John Richard Greene's *Short History of England* and had been impressed by its emphasis on social and cultural material; also John Bach McMaster's *History of the People of the United States* had helped to make him dissatisfied with the purely political narrative. Barnes also suggested that Robinson's interest in the history of ideas was augmented by his reading of the works of John W. Draper, William E. H. Lecky, and Andrew D. White, other and earlier associates of Robinson at Columbia credit much more influence to Henry C. Lea and Lecky than to Draper and White. Robinson's concepts of the new history were further reinforced by his enduring interest in natural science and his interest in the allied social sciences; he had come to recognize that all of these sciences uncovered vast quantities of knowledge about man and his varied activities. He came to look upon the natural and social sciences not as rivals but as allies in the search for truth;⁸⁹ and his broadening interests were reflected in his teaching, his books, and his leadership in the revision of history offerings in the schools.

Thus it would appear that Robinson's concept of the new history stemmed from three main sources: from his desire to improve the teaching of history, his own careful historical investigations, and lastly his

---

86. Robinson and Beard, *The Development of Modern Europe*, 2 vols., Boston, 1907-8. A completely revised edition appeared in 1929-30.
87. See pages 000-000.
88. Barnes, *loc. cit.*, p. 352-3.
89. *Ibid.*, pp. 358-361.

belief that the historian should apply, in behalf of social betterment, the vast quantities of new knowledge being revealed by the allied sciences of man.

After 1912 most of Robinson's professional efforts were confined to interpretating his concepts of the "new history" and its functions. However Robinson retained some contact with historical writing and teaching through successive revisions of his textbooks and through his occasional addresses at meetings of historians. In his later years he planned to write a two-volume book on the intellectual history of Europe, entitled "The Story of Man's Notions of Himself and His World,"[90] but there is no indication that he ever seriously entered upon this project.[91]

In 1929 in recognition of his outstanding achievements as a historian and as a popularizer of the new history, he was elected president of the American Historical Association. In his presidential address, "The Newer Ways of Historians," he reviewed the progress made in American historiography since the beginning of the century and suggested that with the aid of the new allied sciences of man, the historian might look forward to even new fields to conquer.[92] He cautioned his fellow historians, however, not to place too much reliance upon the historical information secured from formal documents, as frequently, in the past, they had presented only the "face and appearance" of things and had revealed little to the historian as to what was taking place beneath the surface. Robinson suggested that the historian in the future might overcome this deficiency by giving more attention to another class of sources, the drama and the novel. He expressed the opinion that the serious description and criticism frequently appearing in the modern drama and novel often presented a very accurate picture of what was really taking place beneath the surface and this would prove of invaluable service to the historian.[93] Robinson had earlier come to doubt, however that the

---

90. Barnes, *loc. cit.*, p. 408.
91. Clifton H. Bushnell, his nephew and secretary, who lived with Robinson for eight years previous to Robinson's death, states that he had never started it.
92. Robinson, "The Newer Ways of Historians," *American Historical Review*, vol. XXXV, 1930, pp. 245-255.
93. *Ibid.*, pp. 254-255. Robinson's interest, at this time, in the value of the modern novel and drama as historical sources was reflected in his revised edition of *The Development of Modern Europe* 1929-30, done in collaboration with Beard. This text contained a twenty-five page chapter entitled "The Study of Mankind in Fiction."

most effective study of man and his problems could be done within the confines of existing academic institutions.

A NEW ADVENTURE IN HIGHER EDUCATION

Just as Robinson's thinking about history had made him a champion of the new history, so did his thinking about contemporary problems make him a social critic. Through his research he had become conscious of what he believed were outmoded and outgrown elements in existing culture. He was repelled by what appeared wasteful, unjust, regimented, or standardized.[94] He had a growing conviction of the fundamental futility and sterility of academic routine and procedure. He felt that the momentous challenge to change man's thinking could be met only by the unhampered use of man's intellect in dealing with current ills, but certainly not in the traditional institutions of higher learning which appeared to him archaic, stereotyped, and circumscribed by rigid curricula, stated examinations, and solemn degree-granting convocations. Even if these weaknesses were eliminated, Robinson felt that the schools and colleges were still unable, because of social pressure, to deal with many of the highly controversial issues concerning the welfare of man.[95]

These convictions led Robinson to speculate with some of his intimate friends, Charles A. Beard, John Dewey, Carlton J. H. Hayes, Alvin Johnson, Thornstein Veblen, Emily James Putman, and others, on the possibilities of developing a new type of institution of higher learning unhampered by requirements, degrees, or other academic traditions, and, most important, free from the numerous repressive influences so evident to him in academic life.[96] Out of these speculations Robinson developed a plan for the New School for Social Research, which was to be devoted to study and research in the field of history and other social sciences. In planning this new enterprise Robinson and his associates conceived an institution of higher learning which would be frequented solely by those who thought they wished to learn and in which there would be no inducement to attend other than the opportunity of learning.[97] Moreover, in order to insure complete academic freedom, especially from administrative repression, Robinson planned to have the

---

94. Barnes, *loc. cit.*, pp. 394-5.
95. Barnes, *loc. cit.*, pp. 339-40. Also letter to his sister Sarah, December 10, 1917.
96. Interview with Alvin Johnson, March 27, 1945.
97. Robinson, "The New School," *School and Society*, vol. I, 1920, 130-31.

New School run democratically by the faculty. There was to be no president, dean, or any of the usual administrative machinery generally associated with institutions of higher learning.[98]

In February, 1919, the New School was opened under the leadership of Robinson as chairman of the executive committee. Quite naturally these new responsibilities caused him to reconsider his relationship with Columbia University. Thus in May of the same year he resigned as professor of European history at Columbia and turned full attention to the New School.[99]

In addition to his administrative duties as chairman of the executive committee he offered courses in intellectual history. Two of his most frequent offerings were The Human Mind and Modern Historical Antecedents of the Present Historical Outlook.[100]

By 1921 the New School was undergoing an internal crisis. The first problem was created by the attempt completely to democratize the administrative machinery. Robinson's original plan to dispense with both dean and president and with the traditional academic hierarchy, and to provide for "just enough amiable administration to transact business and centralize the activities of the school," soon ran into many difficulties. The policy of settling all faculty and institutional policies in an absolutely democratic manner proved so unsuccessful that within a short time it became the source of much friction, discontent, and dissent among the faculty. Dr. Alvin Johnson, a member of the early executive board (and later president), declares that within one year every man seemed turned against every other one.[101]

98. Letter to Sarah, April 7, 1918.
99. The correspondence between Robinson and President Butler of Columbia at the time of Robinson's resignation indicates that Robinson's primary reason for resigning from Columbia was to enable him to give his full attention to establishing and developing the New School for Social Research. This is revealed in the following letters appearing in the Bushnell collection: letter from Butler to Robinson February 10, 1919, letter from Robinson to Butler February 19, 1919. There is no indication that Robinson left Columbia because he felt that his academic freedom had been restricted in anyway. On the contrary, in a letter to Butler February 7, 1919 Robinson thanked Butler for the academic freedom he had been able to enjoy under the latter's administration. Likewise Robinson's letters to his sister Sarah during this time indicate that Robinson was resigning from Columbia in order to give his full attention to establishing the New School. See letters April 7, 1918 and July 4, 1918 to his sister Sarah (Bushnell Collection).
100. New School for Social Research, *Announcements,* 1920-21, pp. 11.
101. Interview with Alvin Johnson, March 27, 1945.

The situation was rendered even less tolerable by the financial problems which soon began to plague the new enterprise. The school had no permanent endowment, and the original pledges of financial assistance had been made for a short time. When these expired, it became increasingly difficult to raise the necessary funds to keep the project going, for the letdown in financial aid was accompanied by a loss of enthusiasm on the part of many of the original workers. The lack of adequate endowment necessitated greater reliance on the tuition paid by enrolled students. Thus was brought to a head the whole question of the purpose and function of the school, on which there had never been complete agreement from the beginning. Veblen had wanted to make it a research institution; Beard was inclined toward a labor college; Robinson preferred to devote it to adult education so that he could reach large groups.[102] Something of the uncertainty as to its future aim and purpose was indicated in one of Robinson's letters to his sister Sarah: "Perhaps in two or three years we may have to alter its object and make it frankly a labor college. But the general public may respond sufficiently to keep it going as it is."[103]

Finally after much discussion, the executive committee decided to reorganize the administrative machinery, to develop a program for attracting more students, and to concentrate on a program of higher education for adults. Robinson expressed a willingness to continue for one year as the head of the school under this new arrangement, but the executive committee decided that this was not a one-year job: rather it would require ten years to establish the school on a sound running basis. This fact, along with his general disappointment in seeing the school deviate from its original objectives, and the fact that he was becoming interested in writing for the general public, led him to resign as chairman of the executive board.[104]

POPULARIZING THE NEW KNOWLEDGE

After Robinson resigned from his administrative position in the New School, he continued to offer occasional classes there for several years. However, he had become convinced by this time that he could perform his greatest service as a teacher by helping to provide books for the in-

---

102. *Ibid.*
103. Letter to Sarah, October 10, 1920.
104. Interview with Alvin Johnson, March 27, 1945.

telligent adult reader, books which would present a clear summary of the progress being made in the various fields of human knowledge.[105]

In 1922, with the cooperation of the Workers' Education Bureau of New York City, Robinson developed plans for editing a series of books designed to help bridge the gap between the new scientific knowledge and popular beliefs. These volumes were to be small, containing from twenty to thirty thousand words, and were to be interesting as well as informing. The series was to be known as The Workers' Bookshelf. A file of the Workers' Education Bureau preserved a proposed list of titles and authors for this project. They were as follows:

> *Humanizing of Knowledge,* Robinson; *Evolution,* Zelong; *Starlight,* Shapley; *The Green Leaf,* McDougal or Spoehr; *The Atom,* Alston; *Spiritual Leaders,* Wells; *Love and Marriage,* Ellis; *Old Age,* Hall; *Economics,* Veblen or McPherson; *Psychology,* Watson; *Communication,* no author; *Human Conduct,* Dewey; *Glands,* Cannon; *Social Life of Insects,* Wheeler; *Magic,* Thorndike; *Psychology,* Martin.[106]

There was also a note at the bottom of the one-sheet prospectus suggesting that Muzzey and McDougal serve on the editorial committee for the project.

Only four of the proposed series were completed. They are *The Humanizing of Knowledge* by Robinson, *Starlight* by Harlow Shapley, *The Green Leaf* by Daniel T. McDougal, and *The Atoms,* by Charles A. Bazzoni.[107] The project, according to Clifton H. Bushnell, was discontinued because Robinson was unable to find suitable authors for the various fields of knowledge he wished to bring before the public.[108]

In his *Humanizing of Knowledge*[109] Robinson asserted that the revolutionary scientific advance of the last three centuries seemed scarcely to have affected man's thinking. This he attributed to the fact that science had tended to develop toward excessive specialization and departmentalization. The result was that the scientists often revealed amazing ignor-

---

105. Barnes, *loc. cit.,* pp. 346-7.
106. This is contained in a typewritten sheet at the Workers' Education Bureau, New York City, (May 1, 1945).
107. Bazzoni was substituted for Ashley as author of this volume. All were published by the George H. Doran Company of New York City.
108. Interview with Clifton H. Bushnell, December 13, 1944.
109. Robinson, *The Humanizing of Knowledge,* George H. Doran, 1923.

ance on problems outside their own subject fields. In view of these defects Robinson suggested that the great need was not to make scientific speculation, research and discovery less extensive or effective but to accompany the process by an intelligent persistent effort to make intelligent adults aware of the great scientific discoveries and their implications. The great challenge, as Robinson saw it, was to bridge the gap between the newer scientific knowledge and popular prejudice which had resulted from ignorance.[110]

Although the projected series of books for adults did not culminate as Robinson had planned, he continued, through addresses and writings, his campaign to bring the mind of his fellowman up to date.[111] The more significant of these later writings and some of the earlier ones were collected and published by Harry Elmer Barnes after Robinson's death in 1936. They appeared under Robinson's name in a volume entitled *The Human Comedy*.[112]

Robinson's restless and quite possibly unsatisfying career as an historian, scholar, and teacher can be divided into three distinct yet overlapping states: that of the young historian primarily interested in historical research, that of the champion and popularizer of the "new history," and finally that of an educator and reformer.

As a young historian in the last decade of the nineteenth century his primary interest was in utilizing the most refined techniques of historical research and methodology to secure the most accurate knowledge of the past. These early interests were reflected in his writings and his classroom activities. His participation in the publication of the *Translations and Reprints* and *Petrarch* were attempts to bring the original source material within the grasp of the student. Likewise he sought every opportunity in his classroom to impress upon his students the importance of original source material in the study of history.

While continuing his efforts to reconstruct the past by using the most refined techniques of historical research, he began very early to reveal an interest in the educational value of history as a high school and as a

110. *Ibid.*
111. Some of the more significant ones were: "Is Darwinism Dead" *Harper's Magazine*, June 1922, vol. CXLV, pp. 68-74; "Freedom Reconsidered," *ibid.*, October and November 1923, vol. CXVII, pp. 577-585, pp. 769-777; "These Eventful Years," *Survey*, October 1924, vol. LIII, pp. 18-21. "How Did We Get That Way?," *Harper's Magazine*, August, 1926, vol. CLIII, pp. 265-272; "The Drift of Human Affairs," *ibid.*, September, 1926, vol. CLIII pp. 426-433.
112. Robinson, *The Human Comedy*, New York, Harper, 1937.

college subject. His own teaching experiences and his many contacts with other historians and educators through various professional organizations caused him to see that the teaching of history needed to be brought up to date and revitalized if it were effectively to serve the educational requirements of our modern age. Robinson found equal challenge from the vast quantities of new knowledge being discovered by the newer sciences of man of which all too often the historian was aware.

His dissatisfaction with the more traditional type of history and his belief that history should be brought up to date led him to champion the more progressive trends of history, namely that history should be more comprehensive in content, utilize more effectively the new knowledge uncovered by the allied social sciences, and lastly select and organize the facts from the past for the high purpose of aiding social progress. These principles he championed through his addresses before professional organizations, his articles appearing in numerous professional periodicals, his history textbooks and lastly through the *New History* which he published in 1912.

After 1912 Robinson gave most of his attention to interpreting the new history. In his famous class in intellectual history, through his books: the *Mind in the Making* and the *Humanizing of Knowledge,* through his numerous magazine articles, written for the public at large, and through his other activities, Robinson had but one aim: to bring the human mind up to date. He came to feel that he could serve his fellow-man best by popularizing the progress made in the various fields of human knowledge and thus make it possible for human intelligence to play more freely on the complex problems facing our age.

What might have been a *magnum opus* in European intellectual history, and which might have integrated the three stages of his career, never progressed beyond the conception of the idea. Two at least of the three stages ended in some degree of frustration. Yet as historian and popularizer, as scholar and teacher, as interpreter, and sometimes as rebel, he left his impression on the minds of those with whom, by a succession of approaches, he succeeded in making contact.

2
The New History

ROBINSON brought to the historical profession not only a thorough training in the latest techniques of historical research and methodology but also a curiosity and interest in fields outside his own profession. His interest in the new discoveries and advances being made in all areas of human knowledge and his association with intellectual leaders outside his own profession, such as E. G. Conklin, Simon W. Patten, Henry C. Lea and William James, enabled him to view the prevailing type of historical instruction with some degree of detachment and to evaluate its effectiveness in the light of the progress being made in the other studies of man. Likewise Robinson, in his own professional field, was in an equally advantageous position. His wide range of studies including government, constitutional law, and the history of man from ancient times to and including the modern period gave him an opportunity to view the whole of human history and to see the vast possibilities and potentialities of historical study. By 1911 Robinson was referring the students in his famous class in intellectual history to the leading thinkers in many fields such as Edward R. A. Seligman, Albion W. Small, Andrew D. White, William E. H. Lecky, George Santayana, Alfred Haddon, Charles Lyell, Maurice Maeterlinck, Edward L. Thorndike, Henry E. Crampton, Margaret F. Washburn, and H. G. Wells.[1]

Although the study of history in both the high schools and colleges had had phenomenal growth during the last quarter of the nineteenth century[2] the methods and techniques of historical study had shown no corresponding improvement. Rather, the study of history, when Robinson began his career, was characterized by outmoded practices persisting from the days when historical study received far less attention.

1. Robinson, *An Outline of the History of the Intellectual Class of Western Europe*, Lancaster, Pennsylvania, New Era Printing Company, 1911, pp. 2-3 and pp. 54-58.
2. *The Study of History in Schools*: Report to the American Historical Association by the Committee of Seven, New York, 1899, p. 1.

The teaching of history in the secondary schools was characterized by the almost complete reliance on a textbook. Professor Rolla M. Tryon described the unique position of the textbook as follows: "During the forty years after 1860 the textbook in history for use in both elementary and secondary schools was 'King of Kings' and 'Lord of Lords.' It was the 'be all and end all' of the content of history taught in the schools of this time."[3] This observation is substantiated by the report of the sub-committee on History, Civil Government, and Political Economy of the Committee on Secondary School Studies of the National Education Association, which concluded that high school history teachers were placing far too much reliance on a few brief history textbooks, and that few teachers revealed either the spirit or resources to carry their classes outside these narrow limits.[4]

The excessive dependence at this time on history textbooks was particularly unfortunate, for they were of poor quality and at best gave only a meager and inadequate view of the past.[5] The writers of texts in European history concerned themselves almost exclusively with political, military, and dynastic affairs, ignoring the other more varied activities of man.[6] At the same time the texts were filled with many meaningless names and dates; they emphasized that which was extraordinary and of passing interest rather than that which was typical and permanent; they neglected causal relations; they projected modern moral standards into the past; finally they gave evidence of the lack of scholarship on the part of the authors.[7]

The textbooks themselves often became the vehicle for the most outmoded and worthless type of teaching; even good teaching was threatened by this excessive reliance on poorly prepared history textbooks. Tryon tells us that in the last quarter of the nineteenth century there remained in the country, "teachers who assigned lessons page by page and listened with textbooks in hand to near-memoriter recitations.

---

3. Rolla M. Tryon, *The Social Sciences as School Subjects*, (Report of the Commission on the Social Studies, Part XI) Scribners, 1935, pp. 154-155.
4. National Education Association *Report of the Committee on Secondary School Studies*, Washington, Government Printing Office, 1893, p. 185.
5. Tyron, *Social Science Subjects*, p. 155.
6. Association of Colleges and Preparatory Schools of the Middle States and Maryland, *Proceedings of the Twelfth Annual Convention*, 1898, pp. 9-11.
7. Edward VanDyke Robinson, "Medieval and Modern History," *School Review*, vol. VIII, 1900, p. 269.

The writer himself has observed history recitations in which the exact words of the author were repeated by the students in recitation."[8] In other classes "learning the lesson" was given a somewhat more liberal interpretation and the student was permitted to give a summary of the more salient ideas appearing in the text material. Very rarely was the text used as a minimum, a point of departure, from which the student was led to an examination and study of other material.[9]

Much of the history in the colleges and universities was of the same general pattern as that appearing in the secondary schools.[10] John W. Burgess in describing the methods of historical instruction used in the undergraduate classes at Columbia, in 1882, wrote,

> Here we employ the gymnastic method and seek the accomplishment of the gymnastic purpose, viz, the daily drill by recitation, question and answer from the textbooks of German, French and English history, and elementary political economy, with the purpose of fixing and classifying in the memory of the student the elementary political geography, the chronology and outward frame of historical events, the biographies of historical characters, and definitions of political and economic terms.[11]

In both the graduate and undergraduate courses, however, there was considerable reliance on the lecture method. The lecture was used in some instances to enrich the text material; at other times the lecture was a mere repetition of what the student had already been assigned to read.[12] The most advanced type of historical study was offered in the seminars modeled after their counterpart in the German universities. Here graduate students were encouraged to examine, criticize, and interpret original source material and to prepare original papers for class

---

8. Rolla M. Tryon, *The Teaching of History in Junior and Senior High School*, New York, Ginn, 1921, p. 55.
9. *The Study of History in Schools*, Report of the American Historical Association by the Committee of Seven, Macmillan, 1912, pp. 144-145, 167.
10. Robinson, "Popular Histories: Their Defects and Possibilities," *The International Monthly*, vol. II, July 1900, p. 54.
11. Herbert B. Adams, *The Study of History in American Colleges and Universities*, p. 77. Quoted from an article by John W. Burgess entitled "The Study of Political Sciences in Columbia College" *The International Review*, vol. XII, April 1882, p. 347.
12. Henry Johnson, *The Other Side of Main Street*, pp. 156-163.

discussions.[13] Such training was, however, reserved for very advanced students in historical study in the United States.

As has already been indicated, Robinson very early in his teaching career manifested an interest in making his classes interesting, vital, and worthwhile. During his second year at the University of Pennsylvania this interest undoubtedly received considerable impetus, for at this time Robinson had an unusual opportunity for a person so new in the teaching profession to view the general status of historical instruction in the secondary schools of the country. This opportunity came when he accepted membership in the sub-committee on History, Civil Government, and Political Economy of the Committee on Secondary School Studies of the National Education Association. Through participation in the deliberations and the final report of this committee, Robinson became acquainted with the more pronounced weaknesses in the history program of that time, such as the lack of clear understanding of the aims and values of history, the excessive reliance upon the textbook and the lecture, the lack of training in the historical method, and finally the lack of uniformity in the history program of the secondary schools.[14]

Although Robinson continued for some time his original interest in historical study, that of recreating an accurate picture of the past through the utilization of the most refined techniques of historical research and criticism, the problems of improving the teaching of history in both colleges and secondary schools came to take more and more of his attention. This interest is manifest in numerous articles in professional magazines; in his addresses to the leading professional organizations; in his history textbooks; in his Committee work; in his university classes and finally in his *New History*[15] published in 1912. He attacked the outmoded aspects of historical study and championed the more progressive trends in history, which he came to call the "new history."

AIMS AND VALUES OF THE "NEW HISTORY"

Indicated earlier, Robinson's career as a teacher of history had two distinct, yet overlapping phases; the first was characterized by Robin-

---

13. Adams, *The Teaching of History in American Colleges and Universities*, pp. 156-162.
14. National Education Association, *Committee on Secondary School Social Studies*, pp. 166-200.
15. Robinson, *The New History*, New York, Macmillan, 1912.

son's interest in portraying objectively the permanent achievements of man by a critical examination and interpretation of the sources; the second was characterized by Robinson's interest in interpreting and in adapting history to what he considered to be the educational and social requirements of the modern age. During both of these phases of his career Robinson concerned himself with the aims and values of historical instruction.

The shift in Robinson's role from that of objective historian of the Von Ranke school to that of champion of the "new history" was a gradual process requiring nearly two decades. In order to trace the origin and development of Robinson's ideas as to the aims and values of the "new history" it is first necessary to give some attention to his early ideas on this question.

At the start of his career Robinson believed that in order to assure history its proper place among the sciences of man and in order to determine the best methods and techniques of historical instruction, the historian and teacher of history must first have a clear understanding of the aims and objectives of historical study. As early as 1894 Robinson noted that there existed an obvious vagueness regarding the precise object toward which instruction in history should be directed; consequently there was uncertainty as to the proper methods to be employed and as to the best selection and organization of the material.[16] Five years later Robinson observed that this condition still existed and that it had an adverse effect on the teaching of history. In an address before the National Herbart Society on the subject of "Medieval and Modern History in the Schools," he made a plea for more careful consideration of the aims and purposes of history as a school subject: "So long as we are uncertain or careless of our aims, our methods of instruction will remain crude and inefficient. . . . It behooves him [the history teacher] to learn what is best worth learning and teach what is best worth teaching."[17]

Once Robinson had determined the crux of the problem, which was the need for a clearer understanding of the values to be derived from historical instruction, he himself proceeded to suggest two major objectives for the study of history. One was that it should provide the student with the opportunity of becoming acquainted with the historical

---

16. Association of Colleges and Preparatory Schools of the Middle States and Maryland, *Proceedings*, 1894, pp. 38-39.
17. *Fifth Yearbook* of the National Herbart Society, 1899, pp. 43-44.

method (techniques of historical research and criticism).[18] The second was that it should attempt to give the most accurate, objective, and comprehensive account of mankind's permanent achievements in all fields of human endeavor—political, economic, social, cultural, and intellectual.[19]

Robinson for nearly a decade seized every opportunity through his addresses to numerous professional organizations and his articles appearing in professional periodicals to call to the attention of his fellow historians and educators the need for focusing their attention on achieving these major objectives. Moreover, Robinson himself through his activities as a classroom teacher and through his publication of source material in the *Translations and Reprints* and in his *Petrarch,* gave concrete demonstration of his belief in the desirability of providing opportunity for the student to become acquainted with the techniques of historical research and criticism. He also at this time attempted to contribute to his other major objective, that of presenting objectively the varied and permanent achievements of man, by publishing his famous text, *An Introduction to the History of Western Europe*.

Prior to this time Robinson's primary concern had been to improve the status and efficiency of history as a science or study of man's past. The methods of instruction and the selection and organization of the material to be taught were to be designed to serve this end. The historian was to be an unbiased observer and recorder of past events. In describing the objective approach of the historian Robinson had written, in 1902:

> The aim of the historian is not to prove that a particular way of doing a thing is right or wrong. . . . His object is to show as well as he can how a certain system came to be introduced, what was thought of it, how it worked and how another plan gradually supplanted it.[20]

However, Robinson soon came to feel that this was not the most important value that could be realized from historical study. It appeared

---

18. Association of Colleges and Preparatory Schools of the Middle States and Maryland, *Proceedings*, 1894, p. 38.
19. Robinson, "Popular Histories their Defects and Possibilities," *The International Monthly*, vol. II, July 1900, p. 54.
20. Robinson, *An Introduction to the History of Western Europe*, Boston, Ginn, 1902-3, p. 3.

to him that the resolution to test one's sources carefully and to state only what seemed to be supported by adequate evidence was, after all, only meeting the preliminary requirements of scientific historiography. The great number of facts about the past of man which were susceptible of satisfactory verification not only exceeded the compass of any single presentation but were so heterogeneous in their character as to invite a great variety of explanations and interpretations.[21] Consequently in 1904—at a meeting of the Association of History Teachers of the Middle States and Maryland—Robinson in considering the place of history in the secondary schools, suggested, for the first time, a new basis for selecting, organizing and interpreting historical facts. He advanced the idea that history, if carefully selected and organized, might be of value in explaining present day problems. At this meeting he urged that the history program of the high schools be rearranged to provide more time for the study of recent history, especially from the middle of the eighteenth century, with the purpose of explaining first and foremost the great problems of the present.[22] Hence Robinson came to feel that the historian must be not only a discoverer and recorder of history but also, through selection, emphasis, and organization, an interpreter of the past for the present.

In 1910, in an address to the National Education Association at Indianapolis, entitled "The Significance of History in Industrial Education,"[23] Robinson developed more fully his theory of the obligation of history to serve the needs of the present. In explaining the role of history in the education of boys and girls attending industrial or trade schools, he gave the following concepts of the relationship between history and present day problems:

> History is what we know of the past. We may question our memory of our own personal acts and experiences. But those things we recall in our past vary continually with our moods and preoccupations. We adjust our recollection to our needs and aspirations, and ask for light on the particular problems that face us. So history in one sense is not fixed or immutable but ever changing. Each age has

---

21. Robinson, *The New History*, pp. 47-48.
22. Association of History Teachers of the Middle States and Maryland, *Minutes* of the Second Annual Meeting, vol. II, 1904, pp. 36-37.
23. Robinson, "The Significance of History in Industrial Education," *Educational Bi-Monthly*, vol. IV, 1910.

a perfect right to select from the annals of mankind those facts that seem to have a particular bearing on the matters it has at heart.[24]

As further evidence of the need for history to shift its emphasis from time to time in order to meet the newer requirements of society, he said: "It is clear that our interests are constantly changing and consequently the kinds of questions that we ask the past to answer."[25] It would seem that the historian, in selecting the history to be taught, manifestly had an obligation to be guided by what the past had to offer in shedding light on the urgent, existing problems.

Robinson proceeded to resolve into its elements an approach in determining the content and emphasis of history courses suitable for potential industrial workers. He suggested the abandonment of the former and traditional concepts of history in favor of the consideration of the needs, capacities, interests, and future careers of the boys and girls in industrial schools to ascertain what was most necessary for them to know of the past in order to be intelligent, efficient, and happy in the life they must lead and the work they must do.[26]

Robinson, naturally following his own suggestions, proceeded to analyze the everyday working conditions of labor. He discovered hard, monotonous, repetitious work carried on in dingy, noisy surroundings. He felt that these conditions of labor denied the worker the joy of responsibility and the sense of achievement which are so necessary in assuring community of interest between worker and employer.

To offset these evils he suggested the aid of history, not that kind of history traditionally found in our textbooks, but those phases of past human experiences and achievement which serve to explain our present industrial life. He advanced the idea that, in fact, history alone could explain the existence of the machinery which the operator must attend. For example, history might well perform an important service by teaching the potential worker how the division of labor, of which he would eventually become a helpless victim, had come about. Moreover, the study of this phase of man's past might enable him to perceive its vast social significance and finally to comprehend the rather hard terms on which things get made rapidly, cheaply, and in great quantities. The potential worker who understood the genesis and de-

24. *Ibid.*, p. 377.
25. *Ibid.*, p. 370.
26. *Ibid.*, p. 380.

velopment of his own impending predicament might, as he grew older, become influential in bettering the lot of himself and his fellows, and finally reconcile economic efficiency with the welfare of workingmen. Thus history might well make an important contribution to much needed social reform.

Furthermore, history, in addition to giving the potential worker an idea of social progress and its possibilities, should be able to furnish for him a background of incidental information which could be utilized in his daily surroundings and which would arouse and foster his imagination by carrying him in thought far beyond the narrow confines of the factory.[27]

In closing his address before the National Educational Association at Indianapolis, Robinson reiterated his belief in the value of history as an aid to social progress by saying:

> Such study will not only meet the special needs of those whose education we are discussing but it will furnish at the same time the best, perhaps the only, means of cultivating the breadth of view, moral and intellectual perspective, and enthusiasm for progress which must always come with a perception of the relation of the present to the past.[28]

Although Robinson had first suggested the possibility of utilizing the study of history in behalf of social betterment in an endeavor to show how study of history could be made significant and valuable to potential industrial workers, he soon came to feel that the study of history might have the same value for society as a whole.

Thus by 1910 Robinson's concept of the aims and purposes of historical instruction had undergone considerable change. He was no longer primarily concerned with presenting objectively the permanent achievements of mankind in the numerous fields of human endeavor. Rather Robinson demanded that the historian select and interpret those facts from the past which would be of most value in explaining the present and in directing human progress. Robinson justified this shift in historical aims by advancing the idea that history should not be regarded as a stationary subject which could only progress by accumulating, criticizing, and assimilating new facts but that history in order

---

27. *Ibid.*, pp. 382-3.
28. *Ibid.*, p. 389.

to achieve its maximum development and in order to secure its proper place in modern intellectual life would have to harmonize itself with the highest aims and ideals of modern society.[29]

Since, according to Robinson, the chief concern of the modern age was to achieve social betterment and progress, it became an obligation of the historian to contribute to this end.[30] Robinson viewed modern society as engaged in a tremendous and unprecedented effort to better itself. He expressed the idea that since intelligent reform depended upon an understanding of existing conditions and opinion, and these could be explained only by following their historical development, the study of history, by explaining the origin and development of many of these problems, might make a valuable contribution toward their solution. Hence Robinson urged that the present, which had hitherto been a willing victim of the past, should now turn upon the past and utilize it in the interest of social advance.[31] The development of a greater degree of historical mindedness, he suggested, would add to our intellectual equipment an element which would be of immeasurable value in promoting progress.

Thus Robinson came to believe that the "new history," by utilizing its refined techniques of historical research and criticism, by freeing itself from the limitations formerly imposed upon it, and by availing itself of the new discoveries made by the allied social sciences, would prove to be of invaluable service in aiding the cause of human betterment. History was to serve the high purpose of helping us understand ourselves, our fellows, and the problems and prospects of mankind.[32]

---

29. Robinson, *The New History*, p. 25.
30. *Ibid.*, pp. 252-253. Robinson acknowledged that history dedicated to the task of throwing light upon modern social, political, economic, religious and educational questions would meet the opposition of some historians. Some, he felt, would declare that recent history could not be adequately written and others would contend that history, selected and organized to serve the needs of the present, would be in danger of sacrificing the principle of scientific abjectivity. See for example Henry Johnson, *Teaching of History in Elementary and Secondary Schools with Application to Allied Sciences*, New York, Macmillan, 1940, pp. 19-24. See also Robert L. Schuyler "Some Historical Idols," *Political Science Quarterly*, March, 1932. However Robinson expressed the belief that these dangers were far less real than those resulting from the historians neglect to utilize historical resources in behalf of the great goal of the modern age, social betterment. *The New History*, pp. 21-22, p. 100, p. 252.
31. Robinson, *The New History*, p. 24.
32. *Ibid.*, p. 17.

THE "NEW HISTORY" AND THE HISTORICAL METHOD

One of the basic objectives of the new history was to offer training in the use of the historical method. As has already been indicated, Robinson, in his own classes, provided every opportunity for his students to examine, criticize, and interpret material from the original sources.[33] He was acting on the belief that only through a careful examination of the sources could the student attain the most reliable picture of man's numerous activities and achievements. It was his conviction that not only did the original sources offer the most accurate information but they also added an eloquence and reality lacking in the secondary sources, which might honestly and dispassionately emphasize and dramatize the great events of the past. Of the significance of sources in teaching Robinson wrote:

> Secondhand explanation usually fails by reason of its want of vividness, and to compensate for this we have often resorted to the merely picturesque, in the past, as the only feasible topic for consideration. We can meet this difficulty by reference to the experiences of eyewitnesses, or of those who lived in the conditions we are endeavoring to impress upon the student's mind. Letters, speeches, memoirs, literary productions can all be employed judiciously. A sermon or tract of Wycliffe or Luther will tell more of the times than a volume of analytical discussion.[34]

A critical examination of original sources would not only assure the most accurate information but would give students valuable experience in interpretation and criticism which experience was of great importance. The failure of many teachers to provide students with such training in skills, Robinson felt, was a serious omission considering the potency of the written word and the general failure of the untrained reader to demand credentials for what he read. If the spirit of blind acceptance of the written page could be discouraged and a critical attitude and discrimination concerning sources of information

---

33. In his later years Robinson expressed the belief that many of the writings of the past classified as literature, especially the novel and drama, would be of invaluable aid to the historian. Robinson, "The Newer Ways of the Historian," *American Historical Review*, vol. XXXV, 1929, pp. 254-255.

34. Robinson, "The Teaching of European History in College," American Historical Association, *Annual Report*, 1896, vol. I, p. 271.

could be instilled in the young reader, history would make a most valuable contribution to education and man's general welfare.[35]

Robinson expressed the idea that teachers of history by neglecting to provide an opportunity for the student to exercise his own faculties in finding material, criticizing and organizing it, was causing history to be taught as mathematics might be were all the problems solved for the pupil. The result was that the requirement for the best grades in history often consisted of an unquestioning receptivity and a good memory. In contrast Robinson suggested that the study of history should bring the student into contact with the actual materials of history. Robinson illustrated his ideas by suggesting that after one year of study the historian should continue as does the natural scientist who after his one year of study often becomes an actual worker in the field. In contrasting the approach in the field of history he said:

> In history, on the other hand, he is informed, but sadly unformed. Not only is he ordinarily excluded from any real participation in the work, but he is not brought in contact with the really interesting and important aspects of the past, but delusively 'prepared' by laboriously learning what most of us teachers have long ago forgotten and scarcely miss. Who of us has, for example, a neat scheme in our minds of the history of the territorial claims of the English rulers to France, from William the Conqueror to the end of the Hundred Years War? We sensibly look it up in a book just before a lecture.[36]

Robinson suggested that if the study of history were to reach its maximum effectiveness and to serve its greatest purpose, teachers should cast aside these traditional concepts and methods; they should aim, instead, to teach the instruments and methods of historical study and to make them contribute to the most fundamental of all arts nowadays, the art of using the best books.[37]

EMPHASIZING THE PERMANENT ACHIEVEMENTS OF MAN

Robinson believed that the prevailing type of history offered in both the high schools and the colleges was falling far short of achiev-

---

35. Association of Colleges and Preparatory Schools of the Middle States and Maryland, *Proceedings*, 1894, p. 44.

36. Robinson, "The Teaching of European History in College," American Historical Association, *Annual Report*, 1896, vol. I, p. 276.

37. *Ibid.*

ing one of the major goals of historical study: namely, the portrayal of the permanent achievements of mankind. This he attributed to three tendencies on the part of historians and textbook writers: the excessive emphasis on political and military affairs to the exclusion of the numerous other activities of man; the excessive emphasis on crises in past human affairs,[38] thus ignoring the law of historical continuity; and finally the inclusion in history textbooks of a great number of insignificant and unrelated facts.[39]

Robinson acknowledged that since history included everything that man had ever said or done or hoped since he first appeared on earth, the historian had a very real problem of selecting from the infinite masses of human experiences those which appeared most significant and worthwhile.[40] The historian and textbook writer, Robinson suggested, should not approach this problem by following blindly the traditional emphasis on political and military affairs but rather should think of history as a science of human affairs that could be called upon to surrender knowledge about a great variety of things of the past. In speaking of this he said:

> If we regard history as the science of human affairs won't it suddenly dawn on us that there are all sorts of things about the past which may be said which have not been said and which perhaps may be more important and more fruitful than everything which finds a place in the ordinary textbook.[41]

Moreover, Robinson called to the attention of his fellow historians the fact that much of the information concerning the political changes of the past, appearing in the current history texts, had come to appear of highly questionable value in the light of many new discoveries. Furthermore, from the standpoint of constitutional, economic, social, literary, religious, political, and artistic changes and tendencies the historian had come to reevaluate many aspects of the past. Many things which at one time had seemed important had, in the light of newer

---

38. Robinson, "Popular Histories their Defects and Possibilities," *The International Monthly*, vol. II, July 1900, p. 54 and p. 62.
39. Robinson, "The Teaching of European History in College," American Historical Association, *Annual Report*, 1896, vol. I, pp. 270-76.
40. Association of Colleges and Preparatory Schools of the Middle States and Maryland, *Proceedings* of the Twelfth Annual Convention, 1898, p. 9.
41. *Ibid.*, p. 17.

knowledge, been reduced to relative insignificance. New knowledge necessitated a reconsideration of the traditional selection and arrangement of the history material appearing in the textbooks.[42]

The newer interests in the varied activities of man, including his social and cultural life, meant that history as "past politics" would no longer suffice. Man had demonstrated his own versatility: he had in the past been more than a warrior, subject, or princely ruler; he had made "voyages, extended commerce, founded cities, established great universities, written and read books, built glorious cathedrals, painted pictures, and sought many inventions."[43]

Historians, according to Robinson, could no longer avoid the responsibility of recording these varied activities of man by claiming, as they formerly had, that the available knowledge of these phases of the past was insufficient for their purposes. Momentous additions to our knowledge by modern historical research and by the new social science allies, especially political economy and sociology, had reduced this deficiency. Therefore it had now become the responsibility of historians to utilize this vast quantity of new knowledge in portraying what to their age and generation seemed essential, the story of man's permanent achievements in all fields of human endeavor.[44]

However, before this objective could be fully realized, Robinson felt that the historian would have to give more consideration to the problem of placing events in their proper historical perspective. This, he observed, was not being done, especially in accounts of Europe's past,[45] accounts which, as commonly written, were concerned not with the normal conduct and permanent past achievements of mankind but, like sensational drama, with the extraordinary, the picturesque, and the lurid. The Middle Ages, the Renaissance, the Reformation, and the French Revolution were often made to appear as a series of events, a record of heroic and shameful deeds; there was no serious effort to portray clearly the essential characteristics of these periods of transformation.[46]

42. American Historical Association, *Annual Report*, 1896, vol. I, pp. 267-8.
43. Robinson, "Popular Histories their Defects and Possibilities," *The International Monthly*, vol. II, July 1900, p. 54.
44. *Ibid*.
45. Robinson stated his belief that the American history texts were much better written than those in European History. Robinson, "Popular Histories their Defects and Possibilities," *The International Monthly*, vol. II, July 1900, p. 54.
46. *Ibid.*, p. 62.

TEACHER OF HISTORY

Robinson, in writing of the tendency to emphasize the drama, said:

> We do all we can to disguise, by studied neglect, the lucid intervals during which a great part of human progress takes place. The dates that we ask the student to learn are those of crisis, or at least of supposed crisis. . . . That these crises are unimportant no one will maintain, but to make them the exclusive subjects of instruction is to sacrifice some of the best and most permanent results to be derived from historical study. The most striking events are not necessarily the most interesting and instructive. On the contrary, their very unusualness is against them in their competition for a place in our program of study.[47]

By giving undue attention to the crises in human affairs, historians had perverted their selection of history and often conveyed entirely erroneous ideas to the students and the reading public. Moreover, they were ignoring the basic law of historical continuity and were also failing to realize that two important changes had occurred, one in people's interests in the preceding hundred years, and the other in our conception of the past so modified by recent discoveries that many important matters had been put in an entirely new light.[48]

If the "new history" was going to achieve its goal of portraying the major achievements of mankind in their appropriate historical perspective, two related innovations in historical presentation would be required: first, an exposition of the habitual conduct of mankind during each period of history, not simply a recounting of man's exceptional, abnormal performances and the disasters which have overtaken him from time to time; second, a discontinuance of over-emphasis on the crises in human affairs to the sacrifice of the transitional periods of history.[49]

The historian, endeavoring to describe the more significant achievements of mankind, should recognize the fact that teaching a series of unrelated facts—dates, names, battles, and decrees—, as was often done in introductory courses in history, was largely a waste of time.[50] Studying for the primary purpose of gaining an encyclopedic knowledge had become an anachronism in the midst of our many books of

---

47. American Historical Association, *Annual Report*, 1896, p. 268.
48. *Fifth Yearbook* of the National Herbart Society, 1899, p. 44.
49. Robinson, "Popular Histories their Defects and Possibilities," *The International Monthly*, vol. II, July 1900, p. 62.
50. American Historical Association, *Annual Report*, vol. I, 1896, p. 78.

ready reference.⁵¹ Also, the "new history" should emphasize conditions as well as events. This new emphasis should be accompanied by a more careful selection of facts for discussion, facts discriminatingly selected to illustrate and explain past conditions that would otherwise be but little understood. By eliminating many of the insignificant but commonly taught facts which might well be looked up in a reference book, Robinson hoped to secure more time for emphasizing the permanent achievements of man. In selecting facts from the past Robinson suggested that a careful distinction be made between two categories: "the relevant, the fruitful facts, facts with corollaries, capable of suggesting deductions, and the kind of dry facts which carry us nowhere."[52]

In 1900 in an article entitled "Popular Histories: Their Defects and Possibilities," appearing in the *International Monthly,* Robinson summarized his views as to what the student should obtain from a course in European history:

> European history should not be regarded as primarily a chronicle of past events nor should it be exclusively or chiefly political. It should, on the contrary, be so treated that the reader might acquire some understanding of the great achievements of Western Europe during the last millennium in *all* the important fields of human interest. The institutions of the past, social, political, educational, artistic, economic, such as the feudal regime, absolute monarchy, the medieval university, the guilds, above all the church must be carefully and sympathetically explained, for otherwise history becomes a mere confusion of names and dates. The Middle Ages, the Renaissance, Reformation and Revolution should be dealt with not as a series of events but . . . with the aim of making clear the nature and spirit of each. Transitional periods during which a great part of human progress is made should be given due consideration. The importance of past facts should no longer be measured by the traditional popular standards of conspicuousness but should be so selected and presented as to increase and clarify the reader's understanding of the prevailing conditions of a given period.[53]

51. *Fifth Yearbook* of the National Herbart Society, 1899, p. 57.
52. Association of Colleges and Preparatory Schools of the Middle States and Maryland, *Proceedings* of the Eleventh Annual Convention, 1897, p. 78.
53. Robinson, "Popular Histories their Defects and Possibilities," *The International Monthly,* vol. II, July 1900, p. 72.

THE NEW HISTORY AND ITS SOCIAL SCIENCE ALLIES

Since history is not only the result of its own long development but is also greatly affected by the general status of contemporaneous knowledge and interests, Robinson found a unique situation confronting the modern historian, a most favorable position to explore fruitfully the past because of the availability of an unprecedented amount of information concerning man and his varied activities.[54] Most of this vast amount of knowledge was of recent origin, the worthy contribution of the newer sciences of man such as anthropology, archaeology, social and animal psychology, political economy, and comparative religion. Quite naturally these newer discoveries profoundly affected many concepts formerly held by the historian and the general public. A notable example was the archaeological discoveries uncovering vast new sources of reliable information about the remote past, thus shifting the implication of *prehistoric* from the time immediately before Homer and Moses to thousands of years before them. Equally significant were the contributions of other social scientists, all of whom studied man in their own peculiar way. Their discoveries not only changed the meaning of such words as *race, religion, progress,* the *ancients, culture,* and *human nature,* but also served to explain historical phenomena which the historian could not possibly have rightly interpreted with the means formerly at his disposal.[55]

Instead of considering these discoveries an intrusion, the historian should welcome all available information on the past of man regardless of the nature of the sources. Under no circumstances should the student of the past set his study off as a separate discipline and attempt to defend it against seemingly hostile sciences. Any attempt to do this would be to misapprehend the basic conditions of scientific advance and to ignore the fact that the bounds of all departments of human research and speculation are inherently provisional, indefinite, and fluctuating. Furthermore, their lines of demarcation are hopelessly interlaced, for real men and the real universe in which they live are so intricate as to defy all the most patient and subtle attempts to separate them.[56]

In further evaluating the significance and importance of history's

---

54. *The New History*, pp. 70-71.
55. *Ibid.*, pp. 83-85.
56. *Ibid.*, p. 73.

newly acquired allies, Robinson suggested that the new history, to reach its highest development, must surrender all its individualistic aspirations and must recognize that it is but one of several ways of studying mankind. It must confess that, like geology, biology, and most of the other sciences, it is dependent upon its sister sciences and that it can progress only with them. Since history is always concerned with man himself, the historian would be foolish and arrogant to neglect the various discoveries made about man by those who study him in ways different from the traditional.[57]

Robinson, quite obviously recognizing the impossibility of the historian's keeping up with developments in all branches of the other social sciences, suggested that the best the historian could hope to do was to master a few of the elements of the science most nearly allied to his own. It was equally apparent that the historian might use anthropological and psychological discoveries and information without becoming an anthropologist or a psychologist. These discoveries inevitably suggested new points of view and new interpretations to the historian and in turn helped him to rectify old errors and to dispel immeasurably ancient illusions that still permeated historical studies.

Lest the historian become discouraged by the seemingly prolific output of the other sciences, Robinson consoled him by admitting that speculation in the newer fields of study had often outrun the accumulated data and also that the historical student had often been offered explanations of the past which he had done well to reject.[58] "The sociologist, anthropologist, and economist have doubtless often thought too fast and too recklessly, and this has engendered an excessive reserve in the historian, who has sometimes flattered himself on not thinking at all."[59] Robinson recognized the risks of both paths but believed that in the long run there is more risk in thinking too little than too much.[60] Furthermore, the kind of thought suggested by these new allies of history should serve, if judiciously profited by, to strengthen and deepen the whole range of historical study and to render its results far more valuable than they had hitherto been.[61]

Thus it would appear that while many of the historians of his day

57. *Ibid.*, p. 74.
58. *Ibid.*, p. 100.
59. *Ibid.*
60. *Ibid.*
61. *Ibid.*

were bewildered by the unprecedented amount of knowledge being turned out by the newer sciences of man, Robinson enthusiastically welcomed these sciences as allies.[62] Moreover, he urged his fellow historians to utilize them for the worthy purpose of creating a more perfect understanding of man's past, which understanding in turn would be the first step in bringing the past into the service of the present.

Thus, the "new history," Robinson believed, should be based as far as possible on consideration of source material, it should provide training in interpretation and criticism, it should dwell on the important and essential facts of man's development, it should emphasize conditions as well as events, it should give understanding of the transitional periods between human crises, of the cultural and intellectual aspects of the past, and should be directed to the understanding of the present and its problems.

PROMOTING THE "NEW HISTORY" THROUGH ADDRESSES AND WRITINGS

Robinson not only expounded but actively championed the newer concepts of history in his addresses and articles and in the *New History* which, in 1912, brought together earlier statements in one volume. He reached, variously, college and university scholars, secondary-school teachers, and organizations of administrators and other educators with a range of interests and specializations. As might be expected the same ideas were often repeated to his changing audience.

The first professional organization in which Robinson advocated some of the basic principles of the "new history" was the Association of Colleges and Preparatory Schools of the Middle States and Maryland, an organization composed of teachers and administrators from colleges, private preparatory schools, and public high schools. In 1894 Robinson participated in a general discussion of the "Place and Teaching of History and Politics in Schools and Colleges"[63] at a meeting of this association held at Johns Hopkins University. At this meeting, in a paper entitled "Ought the Sources To Be Used in the Teaching of History?" Robinson first advanced views on the importance of

---

62. *Ibid.*, pp. 70-71.
63 Association of Colleges and Preparatory Schools of the Middle States and Maryland, *Proceedings*, 1894, pp. 38-44. See above, p. 00.

sources and historical method which were later repeated in addresses to other groups.

Robinson suggested to his fellow historians and educators that there should be a much greater use of the sources in teaching history, to add vividness and reality to the study and provide the student with instruction in the use of the historical method. The latter, by giving the student an opportunity to examine, criticize, and interpret a variety of materials, would be of invaluable aid in developing in the student a healthy skepticism and critical judgment of written records.[64] In 1897, before the same association, Robinson reiterated his belief that the student should be taught the historical method in both the high school and college. At this meeting a question was raised as to what the Committee on History, Civil Government, and Political Economy (1892)[65] meant when it had recommended that in the eighth year of history study a special period of history be studied in an intensive manner. Robinson asserted that this most certainly did not mean that the high school student was expected to undertake original research but that it did suggest that in studying history the student should be given the opportunity to exercise his own faculties in finding material, criticizing and organizing it. History might then become an effective vehicle for teaching students to use discrimination and judgment in evaluating facts. Thus the student would complete his high school study with the conception of history as being a stimulus to clear thinking and objective investigation, not an inflexible, dogmatic statement of facts.[66]

At this meeting he also first urged the teachers of history to be more careful in their selection of facts, reminding them that since the history teacher worked with the student for such a short time, the teacher should choose for study only the most fruitful facts.

The following year, 1898, at another meeting of the Association of Colleges and Preparatory Schools of the Middle States and Maryland, in a general discussion on "The Teaching of History in the Secondary Schools," Robinson again emphasized the need for a more careful

64. Association of Colleges and Preparatory Schools of the Middle States and Maryland, *Proceedings* of the Eleventh Annual Convention, 1897, pp. 77-79.

65. This was part of the general *Report of the Committee on Secondary School Studies* of the National Educational Association of 1892, in which Robinson participated.

66. Association of Colleges and Preparatory Schools of the Middle States and Maryland, *Proceedings* of the Eleventh Annual Convention, 1897, p. 78.

selection of facts to be taught. He also urged his fellow historians and writers of textbooks to break from the conventional themes of military and political affairs and to give more attention to the social, economic, and intellectual activities of man.[67]

Robinson, after helping in 1903 to organize the Association of History Teachers of the Middle States and Maryland,[68] became very active in this organization, particularly in promoting his concepts of the new history. In 1904 he served as a member of a special committee established by the association to study and report on college entrance requirements; in 1906 he became its fourth president;[69] in 1909 he addressed the Seventh Annual Convention on "How to Make History More Definite";[70] in 1925 he addressed the annual convention on the subject, "Some Fruits of Historical Study."[71] In all of these activities Robinson urged the need for selecting and interpreting the facts of the past for the benefit of the present.

Also in his addresses before other professional organizations, especially the American Historical Association, Robinson continued his campaign for a new and revitalized history. In 1896 he addressed the American Historical Association on "Teaching of European History in College."[72] At this time he stated many of the basic concepts of the "new history." These were the elimination from the history textbooks of many of the worthless facts that drew attention from the permanent achievements of man, the necessity of providing opportunity for the students to become familiar with the historical method, and lastly the necessity for increasing the scope of history to include, besides the political, the economic, social, literary, religious, and artistic changes and tendencies.

In 1910 Robinson again read an important paper before the American Historical Association entitled "The Relation of History to the

67. Association of Colleges and Preparatory Schools of the Middle States and Maryland, *Proceedings* of the Twelfth Annual Convention, 1898, pp. 8-12. See above, p. 34.
68. Association of the History Teachers of the Middle States and Maryland, *Proceedings*, 1933, p. 3.
69. Association of History Teachers, *Minutes* of Second Annual Meeting, 1904, pp. 30-40. See page 00 for further discussion of his activities on this committee.
70. Association of History Teachers, *Seventh Annual Convention*, 1909, pp. 6-12.
71. Association of History Teachers, *Proceedings*, 1925, pp. 74-78.
72. American Historical Association, *Annual Report*, vol. I, pp. 267-276. See above, pages 40, 43, and 44.

Newer Sciences of Man."[73] In this address he urged his fellow historians to welcome help from the new sciences of man and suggested that if history were to reach its highest development, it must surrender all individualistic aspirations and recognize that it was but one of the several ways of studying man. In speaking of the desirability for the historian to utilize the newer knowledge derived from the other sciences, Robinson said: "In short, whatever history may or may not be, it always concerns itself with man. Would it not be the height of folly and arrogance for the historian to neglect the various discoveries made about man by those who study him in ways different from those of the traditional student."[74] This relation of the sciences of man seemed to Robinson especially important because of the fact that some of the more recent discoveries had invalidated many of the cherished conclusions of historians and had served to explain historical phenomena which the historian could by no possibility have rightly interpreted with the means at his disposal. Thus many of the new discoveries would inevitably suggest new points of view and new interpretations to the historians and would help to correct many of the false conclusions previously drawn.[75]

Although Robinson was most active in the American Historical Association, the Association of Colleges and Preparatory Schools of the Middle States and Maryland, and the Association of History Teachers of the Middle States and Maryland, he reached many other educators and historians through his addresses to other organizations and through his writings. For example, in 1898 Robinson spoke before the National Herbart Society on the subject of "Medieval and Modern History in the Schools."[76] In this address he repeated, for his new audience, his earlier demands (made in the American Historical Association and the Association of Colleges and Preparatory Schools of the Middle States and Maryland)[77] for a clearer definition of the aims and objectives of historical study, for a

73. *Journal of Philosophy, Psychology and Scientific Methods*, vol. VIII, March 1911, pp. 141-157. This was the basis for the chapter on "The New Allies of History" in the *New History*.
74. *Ibid.*, p. 144; *New History*, p. 74.
75. *Journal of Philosophy, Psychology and Scientific Methods*, vol. VIII, p. 157; *New History*, p. 83.
76. *Fifth Yearbook* of the National Herbart Society, 1899, pp. 42-68. See above page 43.
77. American Historical Association, *Annual Report*, 1896, vol. I, pp. 267-276 and the Association of Colleges and Preparatory Schools of the Middle States and Maryland, *Proceedings* of the Twelfth Annual Convention, 1898, pp. 8-12.

TEACHER OF HISTORY   51

more careful selection of the facts to be taught, and for less emphasis on the dramatic episodes of the past.

Two years later, in 1900, Robinson published in the *International Monthly* the article entitled "Popular Histories: Their Defects and Their Possibilities,"[78] which summarized to a large degree his earlier criticisms of the traditional type of historical study and his suggestions for improving it.

In 1910, as has been indicated earlier, he made one of his most important addresses, "The Significance of History in Industrial Education,"[79] at a meeting, in Indianapolis, of the superintendents of large city schools, sponsored by the National Education Association. In this address Robinson emphasized the fact that history was not immutable but rather a subject that should be changed to suit the needs and requirements of our present age. Therefore educators should abandon the traditional concepts of history in developing a program of historical study and should aim to present those facts from the past which would help the students understand the present. Moreover, historical study should attempt to interpret the past for the benefit of the present and for the high purpose of aiding social progress.

Finally, in 1912, Robinson published his *New History*,[80] which summarized the basic concepts that Robinson had championed for the previous two decades. Most of the essays appearing in this volume had been printed before as addresses or contributions to periodicals.[81] However, they were revised and adjusted to make the volume more coherent. Over five thousand copies of this book were printed,[82] and it came to play an important part in every serious discussion of the teaching of history that followed.[83]

78. Robinson, "Popular Histories: Their Defects and Their Possibilities," *The International Monthly*, vol. II, July 1900, pp. 47-73. See above, pages 42 and 45.
79. Robinson, "The Significance of History in Industrial Education," *Educational Bi-Monthly*, vol. IV, 1910, pp. 376-389. See above, pp. 35-7.
80. J. H. Robinson, *The New History*, New York, Macmillan, 1912. The "New History" was the title of Edward Eggleston's presidential address before the American Historical Association in 1900. This address called for a new type of history with less emphasis on military exploits and political activities. The high aim of the study of history, according to Eggleston, was the making of good men and good women. American Historical Association, *Annual Report*, vol. I, 1900, pp. 237-47.
81. *The New History*, Preface.
82. Letter from Publisher, August 28, 1944.
83. It formed the basis of a large part of the discussion of the Committee on

Thus Robinson through his addresses to professional organizations, through his writings in professional periodicals, and lastly through his publication of the *New History* endeavored to arouse his fellow historians and other educators to the need for reconsidering the aims, objectives, and methods of historical study and for bringing them into line with the newer educational requirements of our modern age.

PROMOTING THE CONCEPTS OF "NEW HISTORY" THROUGH PROFESSIONAL COMMITTEES

Robinson, in addition to championing the newer concepts of history through his contributions to professional periodicals and through addresses to professional organizations, exerted considerable influence on the teaching of history by actively participating in the deliberations of several professional committees which were considering the place and function of history in the schools. These were the Sub-committee on History, Civil Government, and Political Economy of the Committee on Secondary School Studies of the National Education Association, 1892;[84] a special committee on college-entrance requirements of the Association of History Teachers of the Middle States and Maryland, 1904;[85] the Committee of Five of the American Historical Association, 1911;[86] and the Committee on the Social Studies of the Commission on the Reorganization of Secondary Education appointed by the National Education Association, 1916.[87]

Robinson's first opportunity to examine the type of history being offered in the secondary schools came in 1892 when he accepted membership on the Sub-committee on History, Civil Government, and Political Economy of the Committee on Secondary Education and participated in the deliberations and final report. The work of this sub-com-

---

the Social Studies of the Commission on the Reorganization of Secondary Education, 1916. It is also treated in books on the teaching of history and social studies by such as Henry Johnson, *Teaching of History*, New York, Macmillan, 1915; Edgar B. Wesley, *Teaching of the Social Studies*, Boston, Heath, 1937.

84. National Education Association, *Report of the Committee on Secondary School Studies*, Washington, Government Printing Office, 1892, pp. 162-210.

85. Association of History Teachers of the Middle States and Maryland, *Minutes* of the Second Annual Meeting, vol. II, pp. 30-38.

86. American Historical Association, *The Study of History in Secondary Schools*, Macmillan, 1912.

87. *The Social Studies in Secondary Education*, U. S. Bureau of Education, Bulletin No. 28, 1916.

mittee, which met in Madison, Wisconsin, in December, 1892, marked the first important effort of any organization to evaluate the work being done in the secondary schools and to make comprehensive recommendations for the future. After carefully surveying the conditions relating to the teaching of history, the subcommittee made recommendations covering a wide range of problems. Suggestions were formulated for a history program in both elementary and secondary schools; discussions were on such problems as allocation of school time to history, the interrelationship of subjects, teaching methods and techniques, and the training of teachers.[88] Records are not available to establish what specific part Robinson played in the deliberations and final recommendations of the committee. Of his own participation he said many years later: "In all conferences on historical instruction in which I took part, the first in 1891[89] at Madison, I have urged that history for students and readers should always be directed to the understanding of the present conditions and problems."[90]

In 1898 the Committee of Seven of the American Historical Association made its influential report on the teaching of history in the secondary schools. Although Robinson was not a member of this committee, the report reflected Robinson's views on one of the important aspects of historical instruction, the desirability of providing the student with the opportunity to examine, criticize and interpret historical material and the importance of acquainting the student with the historical method or process.[91]

In 1904 Robinson was an active member of a special committee set up by the Association of History Teachers of the Middle States and Maryland to study and report on college entrance requirements in history.[92] This committee began its report by unanimously supporting the recommendations of the Committee of Ten and of the Committee of

---

88. National Education Association, *Report of the Committee on Secondary School Studies*, 1892, pp. 162-201.

89. It appears that after thirty years Robinson had his dates confused.

90. Barnes, *loc. cit.*, p. 393.

91. American Historical Association, Report of the Committee of Seven, *The Study of History in Schools*, New York, Macmillan, 1899, pp. 102-104. In referring to reality and vividness afforded by a study of the original sources, the Committee of Seven cites source material appearing in the *Translations and Reprints* which Robinson had helped to translate and edit.

92. This committee consisted of Austin Scott, of Rutgers College, chairman, E. P. Cheyney of the University of Pennsylvania, J. H. Robinson of Columbia University, W. C. Morey, of the University of Rochester, C. H. Hull, of Cornell

Seven[93] that the secondary-school courses in history should be so organized as to serve in the best possible manner the aims of the secondary school and that no pressure from a relatively few students who expected to enter college should interfere with the service of the whole student body. The committee, although composed entirely of college professors, urged that the teaching of history be so organized that it would be to the greatest advantage of all future citizens, whether going on to college or completing their formal education in the secondary schools, to acquire whatever historic knowledge or feeling that they might come to possess. It was evident to the committee that this was not the current practice, that pressure to prepare a few students for college had caused high schools to modify materially the amount of history taught, the method of presentation, the arrangement of the subjects, and the general value of the study.[94]

After examining various entrance requirements of more than a score of colleges and universities and after observing their effects upon high school courses in history, the committee concluded that entrance requirements vitally affected the work of students who went to college and those who did not. The committee suggested that a solution to the problem could best be arrived at through a discussion of the history courses in both the secondary school and the college. Therefore, this committee recommended that, since both the college and the secondary school teachers were concerned, a committee composed of representatives from each field should be directed to consider the subject of entrance requirements in connection with the general topic of articulation of the courses in both spheres.

Before closing its report, the committee recommended a reorganization of the high school courses in history:

> Your committee, however, in its deliberations was so much impressed with a suggestion of one of its members, made with a view to

University, E. H. Castle, of Teachers College, Columbia. Association of History Teachers of the Middle States and Maryland, *Minutes* of the Second Annual Meeting, vol. II, 1904, p. 38.

93. The Committee of Ten refers to special Committee of History, Civil Government, and Political Economy, a part of the *Report of the Committee on Secondary School Studies of the National Education Association in 1892*. The Committee of Seven refers to the report on the *Study of History in Schools,* Report of the American Historical Association by the Committee of Seven, New York, Macmillan, 1899.

94. Association of History Teachers, *Minutes*, 1904, pp. 30-34.

recasting the forms of the four period-units as the basis of instruction in history in the secondary schools, that it feels in duty bound to present to the association this proposal in the form presented to the committee by the member offering it, and, without any attempt to prejudice the matter, to express the hope that it will be made a subject of careful consideration by the association. As the subject is one of grave importance, your committee would suggest that the author of the proposal be asked to present it to the association at this meeting, in greater detail than in the form about to be offered, and ventures to express the desire that the matter thereafter be referred to the combined Committee recommended in the foregoing report, if such committee shall be appointed.[95]

The first suggested change was that less attention be given to the mass of details in the course in ancient history. Since by the Report of the Committee of Seven in 1899, the scope of this particular course had been extended from the accession of Augustus to the time of Charlemagne (adding eight centuries to this period),[96] many details of Greek and Roman history should of necessity be eliminated. For example, much of the material that had made up the nucleus of classical history and that which concerned the early struggle of the Romans and their civil strife must be sacrificed in view of the wealth of new material and new areas to be covered.[97]

The second recommended change concerned the fields of medieval and modern history: that these be separated, inasmuch as the way they were being taught gave the student no clearer notion of his own times than it did of those of the Huns and the Holy Roman Empire. Through this report Robinson for the first time implied that in the teaching of history more time should be assigned to the present than to the remote past.[98] In the proposed organization the course in medieval history was to include events up to the Treaty of Utrecht or the demise of Louis

---

95. *Ibid.*, pp. 34-5.
96. *The Study of History in Schools*, Report by the Committee of Seven to the American Historical Association.
97. Association of History Teachers, *Minutes*, 1904, pp. 30-34. The necessity for eliminating some details in ancient history was first suggested by the Report of the Committee of Seven in *The Study of History in Schools*, p. 56.
98. This reflects the influence of the Report of the Committee of Seven which suggested that one of the major functions of history should be to prepare students to cope with contemporary problems and to participate forcefully in civic activities. *The Study of History in Schools*, p. 18.

XIV, for these events in a way closed the old regime; the course in modern history was to be expanded into world history and presented during the last year of high school.[99]

The third change recommended was that the courses in English history and in American history, to which the Committee of Seven had assigned a year each, should be merged into a general account of the whole English-speaking people from the time of their settlement on English soil to their occupation and control of that part of the earth which they currently occupied. This proposed change was represented as having two advantages: it would avoid in high school the repetition of American history in a form similar to that universally taught in grammar school; it would save a year which, by this amalgamation, could be utilized for a new course.

The fourth innovation was the recommendation of a history of the world from a European standpoint, the time to include events from the middle of the eighteenth century, the purpose to explain first and foremost the great problems of the present. This course would embrace not only political affairs but also the elements of economics, economic geography, and the progress of applied science. Such broad content would create substantial basis for further study in any of these various fields.[100]

As the last suggestion the committee proposed that, when the study of history for four years was inexpedient, a two year course based upon the recent history of the world could properly follow a revised course on ancient history.[101]

The four-year program for high school appeared as follows:

First year: Ancient history—to Charlemagne
Second year: Medieval history to the Treaty of Utrecht or the demise of Louis XIV
Third year: Combination English and American History
Fourth year: World history, since the middle of the eighteenth century, from a European standpoint.[102]

---

99. Association of History Teachers. *Minutes*, 1904, pp. 36-7.
100. *Ibid.*, p. 37.
101. *Ibid.* It is interesting to note that the Committee of Five in its report to the American Historical Association (*The Study of History in Schools*, 1911), of which Robinson was a member, dropped medieval history as such from the program and gave modern history more emphasis.
102. Associations of History Teachers, *Minutes*, 1904, pp. 34-37.

There is no doubt that the proposed plan for reorganizing the history program of the secondary school was Robinson's, and that he had been the one who originally proposed it to the committee. This conclusion is borne out by the fact that, in the general discussion which followed, the proposal was referred to as "Robinson's scheme" and that Robinson was the only member of the committee called upon to explain the suggested changes in more detail.[103]

Robinson's next opportunity to serve on a committee considering the place of history in the secondary schools came when he accepted membership on the Committee of Five of the American Historical Association. This committee was appointed as a result of the growing demand that the four period-units of history, recommended by the Committee of Seven in 1899, be reconsidered and reevaluated. The Committee of Seven (1899) had recommended four period units of history as follows:

1. Ancient history with special reference to Greek and Roman History and the early Middle Ages to 800.
2. Medieval and modern history from the close of the first period to the present time.
3. English history.
4. American history and civil government.[104]

Although the period unit recommendation of the Committee of Seven were widely accepted and became the basis for most of the historical instruction in the secondary schools in the early years of this century,[105] there was, from the first, some dissatisfaction with the blocks recommended by this committee. It was felt by many that ancient and medieval history received a disproportionate share of the time. Also, since large numbers of high school students left school at the end of the first or second year, many were being denied the opportunity of studying any phase of modern history. The American Historical Association, in 1907, acting upon the demand for a reconsideration and reevaluation of the recommendations of the Committee of Seven, appointed a committee of

---

103. *Ibid.*, p. 51.
104. American Historical Association (Report of the Committee of Seven) *The Study of History in Schools*, pp. 34-35.
105. Henry Johnson, *Teaching of History in the Elementary and Secondary Schools*, (1915 edition) p. 148.

five to investigate the situation and bring back recommendations regarding the study of history in secondary schools.[106]

Robinson was made a member of this committee, which later became widely known as the Committee of Five. There is no record of his specific contributions,[107] but there are indications that many ideas previously urged by him became a part of the final recommendations of the committee. One of the first of Robinson's earlier principles to be emphasized by the Committee of Five was the importance of selecting, for presentation to the students, only the most significant aspects of the past. This principle was urged in answer to a general complaint that too much had to be covered in the four-year program recommended by the Committee of Seven. The Committee of Five pointed out that teachers were not expected to cover the whole range of history with equal emphasis upon all events, but rather to select carefully the material for teaching to secure proper emphasis on the more important phases of the past.[108] The committee, in speaking of the history teacher's lack of discrimination in choosing important phases of the past, declared:

> They do not understand that in going over a field they can, by wise omissions and clever condensations here and there, gain time and chance to plough deeper in some portions than others . . . the teacher must use discrimination, be ready to omit unnecessary and unedifying details, pass over unappetizing and unnourishing narrative, and emphasize and illustrate the portions of the field that are especially worthy of study and thought. This process of omission and condensation, of emphasis, and clarification . . . is the process which tries the teacher's soul but it is the essential element of good teaching.[109]

To point to an example of the poor selection of historical material often chosen for teaching purposes, the Committee of Five turned to the area of ancient history. In this area, excessive emphasis was customarily

---

106. American Historical Association, *The Study of History in Secondary Schools*, Macmillan, 1912, p. 4. The Headmaster's Association took the lead in petitioning for this reevaluation.

107. Andrew C. McLaughlin, chairman of the committee, in a letter to the writer stated that he knew of no records and, after these many years, would not care to comment on Robinson's specific contributions. Letter to the writer, April 15, 1945.

108. American Historical Association, The Study of History in Secondary Schools, pp. 19-20.

109. *Ibid.*, p. 20.

placed upon the classical authors and upon the military and constitutional aspects of the past without regard to the larger historical perspective and the results of recent historical research.[110] This was exactly the same comment which had been made by Robinson in 1904 in his analysis of instruction in ancient history at the meeting of the Association of History Teachers of the Middle States and Maryland.[111]

Another of Robinson's earlier suggestions adopted by the Committee of Five was that of dissociating the study of medieval and modern history. The Committee of Seven had combined medieval history and modern history and had recommended that the two be taught as one course in the third year of secondary school; the Committee of Five, following the recommendations made by Robinson, in 1904 separated the two and urged that more attention be placed on the modern area. The Committee of Five took this view of the situation:

> As the course is now arranged and as it is not uncommonly taught, quite as much attention is given to the Middle Ages as to modern times; in fact, probably many teachers would confess that their pupils know much more of the crusades than of the colonial expansion of Europe, and that Charlemagne and Peter the Hermit are more familiar figures than Napoleon or Cavour or Bismarck. Such a condition can scarcely be justified.[112]

In 1904 Robinson had discussed the problem in this way: "The division Medieval and Modern history, although a perfectly natural one, has one conspicuous vice: as it has hitherto been treated, the pupil comes away with no clearer notion of his own times than those of Attila or Frederick Barbarossa."[113]

The Committee of Five also acknowledged another of Robinson's earlier principles, namely, that students should have the opportunity to handle books and to learn to investigate and discover things for themselves.[114]

The great similiarity between the observations and recommendations of the Committee of Five and some of the ideas set forth by Robinson

110. *Ibid.*, p. 27.
111. Association of History Teachers, *Minutes*, 1904, p. 36.
112. American Historical Association, *The Study of History in Secondary Schools*, p. 53.
113. Association of History Teachers, *Minutes*, 1904, p. 36.
114. American Historical Association, *The Study of History in Secondary Schools*, pp. 14-15.

in the 1904 meeting of the Association of History Teachers of the Middle States and Maryland is obvious. However, this does not appear strange, for at least four members of the Committee, chairman Andrew C. McLaughlin, Charles H. Haskins, James Sullivan, and Robinson had been closely associated in the Middle States Association for several years previous to 1911.[115] In fact, McLaughlin and Haskins presented papers at the 1904 meeting and Sullivan, as chairman of a committee, read a report on "Articulation of Work in History in Colleges and Secondary Schools."[116] Thus it would appear that Robinson's recommendations made in the 1904 meeting of the Association of History Teachers of the Middle States and Maryland had a very direct influence on the deliberations and final report of the Committee of Five of the American Historical Association.

Although the Committee of Five accepted three principles formerly advocated by Robinson, namely, the value of providing students with the opportunity of becoming acquainted with the historical method, the importance of selecting and emphasizing those aspects of the past that would portray man's permanent achievements, and the desirability of giving more attention to the modern period of history, it was in the main an argument for the Report of the Committee of Seven and so had little discernible effect upon the secondary-school curriculum.[117]

The Committee of Five by following the pattern set by the earlier committee ignored the great changes taking place in the secondary schools resulting from a tremendous increase in the number of students attending the high school. The secondary schools which before had been primarily concerned with preparing a comparatively small number of select students for college was now faced with the task of developing a type of general education to fit large numbers of students who planned to terminate their formal education in the high school. Educators became less interested in having their students acquire the historical knowledge and technique required for the college and universities and became more concerned with developing a broader social studies program, including sociology, government, economics, and related subjects

115. The fifth member, Charles W. Mann, died in 1909, so did not sign the report. There is no record of his being at the 1904 meeting.
116. Association of History Teachers, *Minutes*, 1904, pp. 11, 29, 38. McLaughlin and Haskins read papers on Friday afternoon, March 11, while Robinson's and Sullivan's committe report came the next morning.
117. Edgar B. Wesley, *Teaching the Social Studies*, p. 96.

which would acquaint the student with the contemporary world and its problems.

Robinson's concepts of the nature and aims of the "new history" which he had so ably championed through his addresses, writings and textbooks were directly in line with the new requirements of the secondary schools. This led to his being selected as a member of the Committee on the Social Studies of the Commission on the Reorganization of Secondary Education appointed by the National Education Association in 1913.[118] This committee, which concerned itself with the aims, purposes, and general arrangement of history in the junior and in the senior high school, made its final recommendations in 1916 in a pamphlet entitled *The Social Studies in Secondary Education*.[119]

How far this committee deviated from the pattern set by its predecessors is demonstrated in its final report. The program suggested for the four year high school course was as follows:[120]

1. Civics—economic and vocational—one year
2. European history including ancient and oriental civilization, English history, and the period of American exploration, to approximately the end of the seventeenth century.—one year
3. European history, including English history since approximately the end of the seventeenth century.—one or one-half year
4. American history since the seventeenth century, one or one-half year
5. Problems of American democracy—social, economic, political,—one or one-half year.

118. Dr. Thomas Jesse Jones, chairman of the committee, in an interview with the writer, stated that Robinson was selected to be a member of the committee because of his leadership in advocating more attention to contemporaneous life and less attention to the remote facts. Interview, April 3, 1945.

119. A preliminary report was issued by the Committee in 1913. It acknowledged its indebtedness to Robinson for its concepts of history. *Preliminary Statements by the Chairman of Committees on the Commission of the National Education Association on the Reorganization of Secondary, Education,* United States Bureau of Education, Bulletin No. 41, 1913. It also appeared in the *History Teachers' Magazine*, vol. IV, May 1913, p. 136. The final report appeared as the *Social Studies in Secondary Education,* United States Bureau of Education, Bulletin No. 28, 1916.

120. The program was set up on the basis of two three-year cycles: grades 7-9, geography, European history, American history, civics; grades 10-12, European history, American history, problems of democracy (social, economic, and political). This program was adopted with the 6-3-3 plan of elementary and secondary education in mind.

From this final report there is no way of measuring the extent of Robinson's influence on the deliberations of the committee. However, Thomas Jesse Jones, chairman of the committee, believes that Robinson had a profound influence on all the committee's deliberations.[121] His opinion seems to be well substantiated by the report itself, for many of Robinson's earlier ideas of aims, content, and organization of history and the social studies were embodied in it, especially those appearing in the *New History,* 1912. For example, the committee accepted and incorporated in its final report Robinson's statement as to the function and purpose of history in the present age; and it also acknowledged its debt to *The New History* by quoting at length a passage in which Robinson stated that the chief function of history is to help us to understand ourselves and our fellows and to comprehend our most vital problems of the present.[122]

The members of the committee likewise quoted Robinson's statement on changing emphasis in present-day history: "One of the chief problems of teaching history comes from the old ideas that history is a record of past events; whereas the real purpose nowadays is to present past conditions, explain them as far as we can, and compare them with our own."[123]

Later in the report, when the discussion centered on the problem of selecting the facts from the past to be taught, the committee once more turned to Robinson. The members were impressed by his suggestion that in selecting appropriate history for potential industrial workers, the problems should be approached by asking what, considering the needs, capacities, interests, and future careers of the boys and girls, was most necessary for them to know of the past to be intelligent, efficient, and happy citizens. In accepting Robinson's method of approach for selecting the kind of history most suitable for potential industrial workers, the committee suggested that the method be expanded and applied to the selection of materials of history for all children, who, in reality, are "common boys and girls" with interests in the present.[124]

Thus the committee accepted one of the basic tenets of *The New*

---

121. Interview with Dr. Thomas Jesse Jones, April 3, 1945.
122. *The Social Studies in Secondary Education,* United States Bureau of Education, Bulletin No. 28, p. 41.
123. *Ibid.,* p. 42.
124. *Ibid.,* pp. 50-51. At this point the committee quoted extensively from Robinson's chapter on "History for the Common Man" in his *The New History*.

History: namely, history is not immutable but subject to the changing requirements of the age in which it happens to find itself.[125] The committee, following this principle, recommended that the selection of an emphasis on a topic in history should depend upon the degree of its relationship to the present life interests of the pupil or upon its usefulness to him in his present process of growth.[126] Of course, this whole emphasis on the exploitation of the past for the sake of the present had been the essence of Robinson's philosophy for over a decade.[127]

Likewise the committee's recommendation that a course in the Problems of American Democracy (social, economic, and political) be offered in the last year of the secondary school reflected Robinson's ideas as to the importance of familiarizing the student with the contemporary world.[128] Also it gave recognition to Robinson's principle that the story of man's progress and development was not the exclusive task of the historian but one to be shared with the allied sciences of man.[129]

From an analysis of the report on *The Social Studies in Secondary Education,* Robinson's ideas appear to have played an important role in the Committee's deliberations and final report. The many direct quotations from *The New History* reveal that the members of the committees had been influenced by its ideas and that the members were of the belief that it contained the best statement of the philosophy of history appropriate to our times.

The final report, embodying many of the ideas appearing in Robinson's *New History,* was widely circulated by the United States Bureau of Education, some 27,000 copies being distributed in less than ten years.[130] Educators have expressed the opinion that it exerted an influ-

---

125. Robinson, *The New History*, p. 137.
126. *Social Studies in Secondary Education*, p. 41. "Present life interests of the pupil" did not mean what the pupil would himself think of as interesting but was designed to bring the pupil in contact with current conditions, problems, and events: Henry Johnson, *Teaching of History*, p. 65 (1940).
127. J. H. Robinson, and C. A. Beard, *The Development of Modern Europe*, I, 1907, preface. Also Association of History Teachers of the Middle States and Maryland, *Minutes*, 1904, pp. 36-37.
128. Robinson first suggested the importance of familiarizing the students with contemporary world problems in 1904. See Association of History Teachers of the Middle States and Maryland, *Minutes of Second Annual Meeting*, 1904, p. 37, also see above p. 55 footnote 98.
129. See above p. 46.
130. Edgar Dawson, "The History Inquiry: Report of the Directors," *Historical Outlook*, vol. XV, p. 246.

ence on the secondary field closely comparable with that of the Report of the American Historical Association Committee of Seven in 1899.[131] Professor Edgar Wesley says of this report, "Perhaps the history of American education affords no other instance in which so unpretentious a booklet has wielded so great influence upon the curriculum."[132]

Thus Robinson, through his articles and other writings and through his participation in professional committees concerned with the aims, purposes, and organization of history in the secondary school, succeeded in placing some of his basic concepts of the new history into the school program. There remained one other way in which Robinson attempted to place his ideas in the school program: namely, through his textbooks. By analyzing these we find additional and potent illustrations of his attempt to assure the "new history" its proper place among the sciences of man.

131. *Ibid.*, p. 246.
132. Wesley, *Teaching the Social Studies*, p. 97.

3

Robinson's Textbooks

ROBINSON frequently suggested that history teaching could be greatly improved by a more effective utilization of source material and a more careful selection of the facts to be taught. His interests lay in having the students examine the original sources at first hand, and in the desirability of having the students analyze and criticize historical evidence. So, as his first publishing venture he was led to edit volumes which would present in collected and convenient form source material suitable for college-level use, and, later to publish history textbooks which would apply his theories, which have been summarized in the previous chapter. Consequently he initiated, with his colleagues, Cheyney, Munro, and later Whitcomb an authoritative history series entitled *Translations and Reprints from the Original Sources of European History*.[1] This series, according to Harry Elmer Barnes, represented the first serious and important effort in this country to introduce source material in the college teaching of general European history.[2] This work consisted of a series of pamphlets, later bound in book form, from twenty to thirty-five pages long and selling for ten to twenty-five cents each. It contained translations and reprints of a number of important original source documents, the use of which would make the study of history more tangible. Robinson, as noted earlier, himself contributed the following: "Protest of the Cour des Aides of Paris," "French Revolution," "Napoleon and Europe," "Period of the Early Reformation in Germany," "Pre-Reformation Period," and "The Restoration and the European Policy of Metternich."[3] His primary purpose was to make available for his own history classes a more adequate and accessible supply of

1. *Translations and Reprints from the Original Sources of European History*, I-V. Department of History of the University of Pennsylvania, 1894-99. Cheyney, Munro, Whitcomb, and Robinson worked on this enterprise together, each editing the material from his own particular field of specialization.
2. H. Odum, *American Masters of the Social Science*, p. 328. Actually Ernest F. Henderson published *Selected Documents of the Middle Ages*, London, George Bell and Sons, in 1892.
3. *Translations and Reprints*, I-V.

source material.[4] Regarding the importance of source material for students, he wrote that the only history worth reading was that which came from the mouths of those who made or saw it. He further observed:

> The sequence of past events, the form and spirit of institutions, the characters of men, the prevailing habit of thought obtain the greatest realities when we study them in the very words used by the men to whom the past was a living present. . . . One fresh draught of such history is worth more than a thousand volumes of abstract reasoning, suppositions and theories. . . . Experience has proved not only that interests of the student can be readily obtained through the vividness of a direct and firsthand presentation, and that knowledge thus gained is more tangible and exact; but that critical judgment is developed in no slight degree, and the ability as well as interest for further study thus secured.[5]

The need for placing source material in such convenient form that it was easily available to a large number of students was indicated by the immediate popularity of the *Translations and Reprints*. As early as 1895, one year after the project was started, the early numbers were being used in sixteen colleges and universities, in some "lower" schools, and in extension and general reading courses.[6]

In 1898, Robinson, with the collaboration of Henry W. Rolfe,[7] made other sources accessible by publishing *Petrarch: The First Modern Scholar and Man of Letters*.[8] This work consisted largely of a selection of Petrarch's correspondence with Boccaccio and other friends, translated from the original Latin, and selected and designed to illustrate the beginnings of the Renaissance. *Petrarch* was well received and generally accepted as a distinct contribution to the better understanding of the intellectual climate at the beginning of the Renaissance.[9]

However, Robinson soon perceived that, although the utilization of source material was important in illuminating the past, what was really

---

4. *Ibid.*, I, No. 3, Introductory note.
5. *Ibid.*
6. *Ibid.*
7. Professor Henry W. Rolfe, an intimate friend of Robinson's and a professor of Latin at Swarthmore College.
8. J. H. Robinson, *Petrarch: The First Modern Scholar and Man of Letters*. Translated with Henry W. Rolfe, New York, Putnam, 1898.
9. In the Bushnell collection there are over forty reviews praising the work as a real aid in illuminating the early Renaissance. Robinson made two other contribu-

TEACHER OF HISTORY 67

needed to improve the teaching of history was a reconsideration and a re-evaluation of the facts commonly included in high school and college manuals. On many occasions he expressed the opinion that history texts, especially in the field of European history, appeared to be filled almost exclusively with discussions of political and military events, with insignificant and unrelated facts, instead of with the story of man's permanent achievements, his varied activities and accomplishments.[10]

TEXTS FOR COLLEGE USE

Finally, after criticizing for several years the traditional type of text in European history, Robinson published his distinguished *An Introduction to the History of Western Europe*.[11] In its preface he reiterated that selection was one of the most important functions of the historian and explained the basis for his own choice of the material in this text. The first problem that he had tried to resolve was the fundamental one of proportion, to bring the narrative into harmony with the most recent conceptions of the relative importance of past events and institutions. Needless to say, this process had required the omission of the names of many personages and numerous incidents and events traditionally found in historical manuals but adding nothing to the students' understanding of the subject. The space saved by these omissions was utilized for three main purposes: first, a much fuller discussion than usual of the institutions under which Europe had lived for centuries, above all the Church; second, inclusion of the lives and work of a few men of foremost importance in the various fields of human endeavor, treated proportionately to their significance in the world; third, the inclusion of not only political but also economic, intellectual, and artistic achievements of the past, so broad in scope as to form an integral part of the narrative.[12]

---

tions of source material; *Readings in European History*, New York, Ginn, 1904 and 1906, 2 vols. and *Readings in Modern European History* (in collaboration with Charles A. Beard), New York, Ginn, 1908, 2 vols. These were designed to accompany the author's college texts in the respective fields. See pp. 79 and 84.

10. Association of Colleges and Preparatory Schools of the Middle States and Maryland, *Proceedings* of the Twelfth Annual Meeting, 1898-9, and J. H. Robinson "Popular Histories: Their Defects and Possibilities," *The International Monthly*, vol. II, July 1900, p. 54.

11. Robinson, *An Introduction to the History of Western Europe*, Boston, Ginn, 1902-3, Preface.

12. *Ibid*. Preface.

The first marked innovation in Robinson's book was the application of his first chapter to an explanation of the historical point of view.[13] He acknowledged that history, in reality, is a limitless science of past human affairs, a subject immeasurably vast and important but exceedingly vague.[14] Choosing from this illimitable past, his text had for its objective the description of the most significant achievements of Western civilization during the past fifteen hundred years. Therefore, the book would take cognizance of man's habitual conduct, of those things that he kept on doing in essentially the same manner for a century or so. Therefore, particular events would be given consideration only in so far as they illustrated these relatively permanent conditions and explained how the Western world passed from one state to another.

In another statement the author suggested that institutions and beliefs which were different from ours should be studied sympathetically; the aim of the historian is not to prove that a particular way of doing a thing is right or wrong, but to show as well as he can how a certain system came to be introduced, what was thought of it, how it worked, and how another plan gradually supplanted it.[15]

Robinson also called attention to the general continuity of history, to the fact that all great changes have come slowly, and that at no time in the past have all the customs of a people been changed abruptly.[16] Thus it was one of the primary aims of this text to show how medieval institutions, habits, and ideas were supplanted, step by step, by those which existed in Europe at the opening of the twentieth century.[17]

Robinson's effort to establish the historical point of view was but one of the many innovations in this notable text. A comparison of it with four widely-used[18] contemporary books will help to determine his other

---

13. The following widely used contemporary texts and syllabi contained no such introduction to the study of history: George B. Adams, *Medieval and Modern History: An Outline of its Development*, New York, Macmillan, 1901. Charles A. Fyffe, *A History of Modern Europe, 1792-1878*, New York, Henry Holt, 1896. Philip V. N. Myers, *A Generl History for High Schools and Colleges*, Boston, Ginn, 1901. Philip V. N. Myers, *Medieval and Modern History*, Part I and II, Boston, Ginn, 1902-3. H. Morse Stephens, *Syllabus of a Course of Eighty-seven Lectures on Modern European History*, New York, Macmillan, 1899.

14. Robinson, *An Introduction to the History of Western Europe*, pp. 1-3.

15. *Ibid.*, p. 3.

16. *Ibid.*, pp. 4-5.

17. *Ibid.*, p. 7.

18. Three of these books: Adams, *Medieval and Modern History*, 1901; Myers, *Medieval and Modern History*; Fyffe, *History of Modern Europe*, were recom-

TEACHER OF HISTORY

unique contributions in the history textbook field. These books are: George B. Adams, *Medieval and Modern History,* 1901; Philip Van Ness Myers, *Medieval and Modern History,* 2 vols. 1902-3; Charles A. Fyffe, *History of Modern Europe 1792-1878,* 1896; and H. Morse Stephens, *A Syllabus of a Course of Eighty-seven Lectures on Modern European History 1600-1890,* 1899.

The first comparison is that of Adams's *Medieval and Modern History* with the contemporaneous text of Robinson as to selection, emphasis, and arrangement of material allocated to various phases of these periods of history. In number of pages Robinson's book was approximately one-third larger than Adams's;[19] therefore when the two authors devoted the same number of pages to a given subject, they were obviously not giving it the same emphasis.

The most important unifying institution of the Middle Ages, the Church, was allotted sixty-three pages in Adams's text, while in Robinson's it received one hundred fifty-five pages.[20] Even allowing for the fact that Robinson's book contained nearly one-third more pages, Adams' text allotted about only three-fifths as many pages to the subject as did Robinson's. However the real difference in their treatment is not fully revealed by the total number of pages devoted to the subject. Of this total of sixty-three pages, Adams apportioned thirty-three to a chapter entitled "The Age of Religious Wars,"[21] leaving but thirty pages to a discussion of the more important features of the Church and its influence during the Middle Ages. On the other hand, Robinson

mended as a select list of books for the study of medieval and modern history in New England History Teachers' Association, *A History Syllabus for Secondary Schools,* Boston, Heath, 1896, pp. 131-141. Fyffe's book was also used as the basis for the course in European History Since 1815 given at Columbia in 1895-96: *Columbia College Catalogue,* 1895-6, p. 81. The fourth book, Stephens, *A Syllabus of Eighty-seven Lectures on Modern European History,* is a second revised and enlarged edition of a syllabus of lectures on Modern European History given at Cornell University for several years. Professor Stephens was one of the influential history teachers of his time and a member of the Committee of Seven of the American Historical Association, (1899). This syllabus is quite in contrast with the syllabus (1901) developed by Shepherd, one of Robinson's early students and later associate. See p. 13.

19. Robinson, *Introduction to the History of Western Europe* contained 687 pages; Adams, *op. cit.,* contained, 458 pages.
20. Robinson devoted ten chapters to various phases of the Church; Adams devoted four to the same subject. Robinson, *Introduction to the History of Western Europe,* and Adams, *op. cit.,* Table of Contents.
21. Adams, *op. cit.,* pp. 228-265.

mentioned the religious wars only incidentally and concentrated on the development of the Medieval Church, its dominant position during the Middle Ages, and the various attempts at reform from within and without. Robinson, instead of making the history of the Church appear as just another series of events, constantly wove his discussion of this institution throughout all the activities of the Middle Ages so that its importance was palpable. However, Adams treated it as merely another topic to be read by the student before passing on to the next subject.

In treating the cultural and intellectual aspects of the Middle Ages, Robinson devoted a total of one hundred nine pages to this subject. Something of the comprehensiveness of his treatment is illustrated by the chapter headings: namely, Culture of the Middle Ages, Italian Cities and the Renaissance, Europe at the Opening of the Sixteenth Century, Germany before the Protestant Revolt, The People in Country and Towns, and Feudalism.[22] Adams, on the contrary, disposed of these aspects of the past in three chapters, The Revival of Learning, The Immediate Results of the Revival of Learning, and The Feudal System,[23] containing a total of twenty-seven pages. Thus, even allowing for the fact that Adams' text was one-third smaller, Robinson's page allotment was proportionately three times that of Adams'. Furthermore, as in the history of the Church, Robinson constantly wove the cultural and intellectual aspects of society into the whole fabric of man's past.

Although Robinson in his text gave much less attention to the economic aspects of the past, and to the life of the common man than he did to the cultural and intellectual achievements of the past, he still treated these subjects more fully than did Adams. However, Robinson's attention was focused upon the economic life of the middle ages with relatively no attention to the commercial revolution and to the economic development of the modern era such as the industrial revolution and the vast number of social and economic problems emanating from it.[24]

Another great difference between the two texts appeared in the treatment of Napoleon and the French Revolution. Adams devoted one chapter of twenty-three pages to this important subject; Robinson, five chapters totaling eighty-one pages. Robinson treated this as one of the great phases of the past, whereas Adams treated it approximately the

22. Robinson, *Introduction to the History of Western Europe*, Table of Contents.
23. Adams, *op. cit.*, Table of Contents.
24. Robinson, *Introduction to the History of Western Europe*, pp. 233-249, pp. 676-677, pp. 680-682.

same as any other topic.[25] Equally significant was the difference in emphasis placed on the various phases of the Revolution. Robinson devoted approximately twenty-five pages to a discussion of the economic, political, and intellectual background of the Revolution, about the same space he had allotted to the period from the meeting of the Estates General to the Reign of Terror in 1793;[26] Adams devoted five pages to his discussion of the background and nine pages to the events taking place between the meeting of the Estates General and the Reign of Terror. Robinson was apparently primarily interested in selecting and emphasizing circumstances and conditions that would best explain events; Adams was obviously more interested in relating the events themselves. This was especially noticeable in the last chapter of the respective texts.

Both authors brought their formal discussion of European history to a close at approximately 1880, Adams adding a final chapter entitled Scientific and Economic Advance Since the Renaissance, and Robinson adding one entitled Europe Today.[27] In his chapter Adams included a variety of topics such as the development of science, the Industrial Revolution and its results, English literature, English Deists, leaders of French thought in England, and French intellectual and social leadership (under Louis XIV). Obviously many of these subjects did not belong under a chapter entitled Scientific and Economic Advance Since the Renaissance. Perhaps Adams had planned to use this chapter to include fragments of information that he had possibly inadvertently omittted from other parts of the text. In any case, the chapter was little more than a conglomeration of unrelated, unorganized facts. On the other hand, Robinson, in his final chapter, organized and integrated his material and appeared to select it with the aim of bringing it as nearly up to date as possible. He included such topics as: modern scientific experimentation, advance in medical science, the factory system, and modern warfare. His discussion of the Scientific and Industrial Revolution explained how many of the modern aspects of our society originated.

25. Chapter on French Revolution and Napoleon contained 23 pages; Chapter entitled France Tries to Dominate Europe; which was really about Louis XIV, contained 20 pages; Chapter entitled The Rise of Russia and Prussia, contained 19 pages. Adams, *op. cit.*, Table of Contents.
26. Robinson, *Introduction to the History of Western Europe*, pp. 536-562. Adams, *op. cit.*, pp. 327-333.
27. Robinson, *Introduction to the History of Western Europe*, pp. 670-687. Adams, *op. cit.*, pp. 445-458. Adams also had a chapter, preceding the last, entitled The Growth of English and American Constitutions, pp. 411-441.

There was no inclusion of extraneous or unrelated facts just for the purpose of narrating them. The recency of his material was exemplified in a brief discussion of the expansion of Russia since the Crimean War, bringing the problem up to 1898, when Russia secured a lease to Port Arthur, and also in a discussion of modern warfare and the prospects for peace, by his including the International Peace Conference held at the Hague in 1899.[28]

A summary of the relative merits of the two texts shows, in the first place, that the failure of Professor Adams to emphasize the Church and the cultural and intellectual life of the Middle Ages, and to select and emphasize those facts which would best explain how things came about were but symptoms of a larger defect, the tendency to include a multitude of facts that did not attempt to present a real understanding of man's permanent achievements. Then too, in addition to cluttering the chapters with many relatively insignificant names and dates, he added at the end of various chapters a long list of "Important Dates for Review," which were to be associated either with some great person or unusual deed.[29] This comparison in the second place, indicates that Robinson's attention to the important problems of selection and emphasis, his willingness to omit many of the facts and names of individuals traditionally included in history texts, and his attempt to discuss the cultural and intellectual aspects of the past, with some attention to the economic life of the middle ages, had resulted in a superior history, one that was truly concerned with explaining man's permanent achievements. However the task of dealing adequately with modern economic history and especially the industrial revolution and the social problems emanating from it was left to some else.

A second comparison is with Robinson's *An Introduction to the History of Western Europe* and a popular text that had just been revised (1902-3), Myers's *Medieval and Modern Europe*, in two volumes.[30] In his preface Myers stated that the emphasis in these revised volumes had been slightly shifted and the narrative amended in the light of recent

28. Robinson, *Introduction to the History of Western Europe*, pp. 686-7.
29. The "Important Dates" are numerous: page 72 contains 28 dates and events; page 155, 45 dates; page 223, 38 dates; page 264, 38 dates; page 326, 35 dates; page 409, 25 dates; Adams, *op. cit.*, the pages indicated.
30. In the preface to vol. I, the author stated that this was a revision of his early volume published originally in 1885. Myers, *Medieval and Modern History*, vol. I, Preface. Part I had a subtitle, *The Middle Ages*; Part II, *The Modern Age*.

scholarly research. He also asserted that purely political, dynastic, and military matters had been subordinated to the religious, moral, intellectual, and social interests.[31] Comparison of the selection, contents, and organization of this text with Robinson's demonstrates to what extent they reached the goals to which they both aspired.

An analysis of the page allotment of the two books to determine the relative emphasis on various major historical areas must take into account the fact that Myers' work contained a total of 1055 pages, and Robinson's, 687 pages, or about one-third less.[32]

Myers devoted a little over one-third as many actual pages as did Robinson to a discussion of the medieval Church, to which,[33] in his preface, he had promised to allocate major attention. Also in describing cultural and intellectual, life, he used only about five-sixths as many pages as did Robinson. Much of this material, moreover, was fragmentary and unorganized, and gave but little concept of the intellectual climate of the Middle Ages.[34]

Probably the greatest difference in the two books lay in emphasis, in the fact that Myers included some material about all phases of the past with no great emphasis to those facts and events which would throw the most light on man's past achievements. There were several illustrations of this, one of the most notable being the emphases that the two authors placed on the French Revolution. Robinson alloted twenty-five pages to the economic, social, political, and intellectual conditions just preceding the Call to the Estates General; and Myers, eleven pages. In contrast to this Myers allotted forty-nine pages to a detailed discussion of various events connected with the French Revolution between 1789 and 1799; and Robinson, thirty-five pages. As for discussion of the French Huguenots, Myers wrote one chapter consisting of nineteen pages, while Robinson incorporated his discussion of them in his chap-

31. *Ibid*. Preface.
32. Thus, if on any topic Myers had about the same number of pages as Robinson, he gave one-third less emphasis to the subject than did Robinson; equal pages would not indicate equal emphasis. Myers, 67 pages; Robinson, 155 pages.
33. This was actually less than one-third, considering that the Myers's total available pages were nearly one-third more.
34. An example of this is his 3½ pages of discussion of the growth of the English language and literature, consisting of the following: effect of Norman Conquest on literature, Chaucer, William Langland, John Wycliffe, and Caxton and the printing press 1/3 page. Myers, *Medieval and Modern History*, Part I, *The Middle Ages*, pp. 386-390. The same kind of treatment is extended to French Literature on pages 401-404.

ter on the Catholic Reformation. Another striking difference in emphasis was in the treatment of the Crusades. Myers devoted thirty-four pages to a discussion of five major Crusades with a mention of some minor ones, in contrast to Robinson's chapter of thirteen pages. In Robinson's text only the most important features of the Crusades were discussed, while Myers considered minute details.[35]

The greatest difference of all lay in the concluding chapter of the two books. Robinson devoted seventeen pages to Europe Today, in which he discussed such topics as modern scientific methods and the new sciences; advances in medical science; science and our daily lives; the application of the machine to manufacturing; new and improved methods of communication; some results of the Industrial Revolution; (the growth of towns, development of *laissez faire,* government regulation of labor, and the rise of labor unions), the growth of democratic institutions; free compulsory education; modern imperialism; and efforts for international peace.[36] In contrast, Professor Myers closed his book with "*Conclusions:* The New Age and Industrial Democracy." In four pages he presented generalizations on these three topics: The Age of Material Progress or the Industrial Age, The Labor Problem, and Socialism or Social Democracy.[37]

The real significance of these differences in selection and emphasis by Robinson on the one hand and by Adams and Myers on the other hand lay in the fact that Robinson, by giving much of his attention to the most important institutions and activities of the past, in reality focused the reader's attention on man's permanent achievements. Both Adams and Myers, by failing to discriminate in their selection of facts, tended to distract the reader and to prevent his gaining perspective in viewing man's great progress.

How far Robinson was ahead of his contemporaries in recording the varied interests and activities of the past may be ascertained by the examination of two widely used histories concerned with the modern phase of history, histories of great popularity at the turn of the century. These two histories are Fyffe, *A History of Modern Europe 1792-1878,*

---

35. Robinson, *Introduction to the History of Western Europe,* pp. 187-200, and Myers, *Medieval and Modern History,* Part I, Note: Myers devoted over three time as many pages to a discussion of the Crusades as he did to the conditions in France preceding the Revolution.
36. Robinson, *Introduction to the History of Western Europe,* pp. 670-87.
37. Myers, *Medieval and Modern Europe,* Part II, pp. 616-20.

and Stephens, *A Syllabus of A Course of Eighty-seven Lectures, 1600-1870*.[38] They illustrate the remarkable amount of emphasis given diplomatic and political affairs even in the treatment of the modern phase of European history.

One of these, Fyffe's *History of Modern Europe, 1792-1878*, dealt almost exclusively with affairs political and diplomatic. In the preface the author stated: "I have occupied myself mainly with two sources of information—the unpublished records of the English Foreign Office and the published works which have during recent years resulted from the investigations of the Archives of Vienna."[39] The content of the book left no doubt as to the sources used; the author never once strayed from them. In no place did he indicate any interest in the social, cultural, or intellectual phases of the past. Robinson's *Introduction to the History of Western Europe* must have appeared a significant and welcome innovation[40] after the narrowness of Fyffe's text.

The other of these histories of the type of history then being taught and written was H. Morse Stephens' *A Syllabus of a Course of Eighty-Seven Lectures, 1600-1870*, offered at Cornell for a number of years.[41] This syllabus of 290 pages treated almost exclusively the political aspects of modern history. Stephens stated:

> The primary object is the study of international relations of the different states of Europe from the beginning of the seventeenth century to the present time. . . . No attempt is made in these lectures to deal with the history of European civilization . . . although political history, when adequately treated, affords man opportunities for dwelling upon the general history of human progress. It has been found of advantage, however, to pause occasionally in the political narrative in order to touch in the briefest possible manner upon the history in literature, philosophy, art and science. Six lectures in three groups are interpolated upon these subjects at appropriate dates. The syllabuses of these six lectures are on a different

38. For its popularity and general importance, see footnote 18.
39. Fyffe, *op. cit.*, Preface.
40. In discussing the diplomatic and political, the author included every detail of which he was aware, and emphasized none.
41. Stephens, *op. cit.*, In the preface the author stated that this was a new and revised edition of the syllabus and that it was published at the request of his students and fellow professors. Stephens was a member of the Committee of Seven of the American Historical Association which reported in 1899.

plan from those on political history, and are intended to bring out the contemporary movements of thought and art through the names of the leading masters, rather than to attempt an exhaustive treatment.[42]

The author stated later on in his syllabus that it contained not only a "mass" of dates but also a "mass" of proper names. To illustrate, he devoted about one-third of his five-page preface to a careful explanation of the origin of our modern calendar and to the spelling of proper names in the various European languages.[43] Something of the value he placed on political and dynastic history was indicated by a twenty-six page appendix attached to his text, cataloguing all emperors, kings, and first ministers of the great and lesser countries of Europe from 1600 to 1899.[44]

This text is not an isolated example of the all but exclusive attention to political, diplomatic, and dynastic history. H. Morse Stephens, the author, was one of the more prominent historians of the last decade of the nineteenth century; his syllabus was widely used and represented the dominant emphasis in American historiography of that time.[45] Only when we come to realize this general condition, do the real innovations of Robinson's text appear in their proper perspective.

Favorable comments on *An Introduction to the History of Western Europe* from the reviewers showed that Robinson's innovations were quite welcome. A review by Paul Van Dyke appearing in the *American Historical Review* characterized Robinson's text in this manner: "In the opinion of the writer this is the best manual of general European history which has yet appeared."[46] The reviewer continued his praise by saying that the two guiding principles, which were so ably demonstrated in the finished product, were omission and emphasis. It was suggested that Robinson's success in omitting many of the less significant details of the past furnished welcome relief to both the student and general reader. Also the book had another important advantage over its predecessors in its emphasis on the non-political and non-military aspects of the past, especially the Medieval Church.[47]

42. *Ibid.*, Preface.
43. *Ibid.*, Preface.
44. *Ibid.*, Appendix.
45. *Ibid.*, Preface.
46. *American Historical Review*, vol. IX, 1903, p. 132.
47. *Ibid.*, p. 133.

George C. Sellery, in a review appearing in the *Annals* of the American Academy of Political and Social Science, was equally enthusiastic about Robinson's new text. This reviewer also recognized as the book's most conspicuous merit its interpretative character, which was achieved by its wise selection of what seemed to be the more important phases of human history.[48]

The *Nation,* in commenting upon his work, observed that the ideals of the artist were much more in evidence than those of the compiler. The author's success was attributed to the fact that he had focused his attention mainly upon the political, intellectual, and economic forces which had step by step transformed Europe. *The Nation,* continuing its praise, stated:

> Selection and emphasis and effective presentation are consequently the keynote throughout. Nowhere has the author scrupled to omit, nowhere spared pains to illuminate. . . . At every step the reader is made to feel that the church was the all pervasive and unifying force of the Middle Ages. There is perhaps no book in English, large or small, that shows so clearly the way in which the Roman Church assumed the discarded function of the Roman State, until it became a great organization, not more religious than political and social—a social organization in the broadest sense, which held western Europe together until the national state system was formed.[49]

Another periodical, the Columbus *State Journal,* characterized the work as a distinctive contribution to historical literature, presenting a readable narrative of the development of European civilization. The real virtue of the book was the fact that the author had dropped the inclusion of the lines of sovereigns and their genealogies and had instead presented the real motifs of medieval life.[50]

The American Hebrew praised the book as portraying a much truer conception of the ideal treatment of medieval and modern history than was evidenced by any of its predecessors. The reviewer also praised Robinson for eliminating a lifeless enumeration of names and dates and for considering the fundamental achievements and institutions of the period covered.[51]

---

48. *The Annals* of the American Academy of Political and Social Science, vol. XXIII, 1904, pp. 165-6.
49. *The Nation,* vol. LXXXVI, June 18, 1903, pp. 502-3.
50. *State Journal,* Columbus, Ohio, June 14, 1903.
51. *The American Hebrew,* New York City, June 19, 1903.

The Catholic Church has been portrayed by Robinson as playing a dominant role in the medieval period; therefore there was a reaction to Robinson's text by a prominent Catholic publication, *The Catholic Mirror.* This periodical had only praise for Robinson's text, especially for the manner in which he had treated the church; "It is an agreeable surprise to find Dr. Robinson so scrupulously fair in this treatment of the church, and at such evident pains to put the facts in their true and proportionate light."[52]

Professor Henry Johnson in speaking of this text said: "*An Introduction to the History of Western Europe* was the greatest piece of textbook writing ever done in this country to that time."[53]

Probably the real significance of the new text was best described by Professor Schapiro, one of Robinson's former students, when he said:

> In his *History of Western Europe,* Professor Robinson produced a history textbook that is at the same time a work of original scholarship. This volume was the first of its kind to give coherence and view-point to complex historical material and to emphasize social and cultural elements. After Professor Robinson, no one may now write an old-style textbook, compendium of dry facts, mainly political and military, hastily put together by a hack writer or a tired historian.[54]

Harry Elmer Barnes, another of Robinson's students and close associates, asserted that *An Introduction to the History of Western Europe* was Robinson's most influential work; for in it he had repudiated the usual assumption that historical material was preeminently constitutional, dynastic, and diplomatic, and had made a positive effort to include, for the first time, much material on economic, social, and cultural life as an integral part of the volume. However Barnes admits that Robinson's chief weakness lay in his failure to appreciate and

---

52. *Catholic Mirror,* Baltimore, Maryland, November 26, 1904. There was some local opposition from Catholic laymen. The Milwaukee *Free Press,* October, 1903, contained an article reciting the complaints of a Mr. Quinn: both Catholic and Lutherans objected to certain passages in the texts: he opposed its adoption by the Milwaukee School Board. The Milwaukee *Sentinel,* October 1, 1903, contained a complaint by M. J. L. O'Connor the passages offended both Catholic and Lutherans. Both of these clippings are in the Bushnell Collection.
53. Interview with Henry Johnson, June 3, 1945.
54. J. Salwyn Schapiro, *Modern and Contemporary European History,* Boston, Houghton-Mifflin, 1918, Acknowledgments.

TEACHER OF HISTORY

to treat adequately the Commercial Revolution, the rise of capitalism, and the Industrial Revolution.[55]

Robinson followed his *An Introduction to the History of Western Europe* with several other textbooks. Two volumes entitled *Readings in European History*,[56] a supplement to his text, were published. These illustrated his emphasis upon the historical and pedagogical value of source material. The source material in the *Readings* was arranged so as to accompany and vivify each chapter of the textbook, a plan to aid the teacher in injecting life and reality to the concepts and generalizations contained in the text.[57]

The success of his first text and his increasing interest in making history divulge what the present desired to know led Robinson into the field of modern history. During 1907 and 1908 Robinson, with the collaboration of Charles A. Beard, published two volumes on the *Development of Modern Europe*.

In their preface the authors stated that they had deliberately subordinated the past to the present with the conscious aim of enabling the reader to catch up with his own times.[58] They felt that in permitting the present to dominate the past they had not dealt less fairly with the general outline of European history during the preceding two centuries than they would have done in merely narrating the events with no practical motive. Also the authors called the attention of prospective readers to the fact that their work devoted much less space to purely political and military events than had commonly been assigned to them. The space so saved was utilized for the discussion of more fundamental matters, such as the Industrial Revolution, commerce and the colonies, internal reforms, and Europe and the general scientific advance.[59] Professor James T. Shotwell, former student and associate of Robinson and colleague and friend of Beard, attributes the increased

---

55. Barnes states that his first edition sold 250,000 copies: Odum, *American Masters of Social Science*, p. 388. At the same time he did not treat adequately the constitutional development of England, this, Barnes suggested, was remedied in his revised 1925 edition. Others noted Robinson's limited interest in English history.

56. Robinson, *Readings in European History*, 2 vols. 1904-6.

57. *Ibid.*, Preface. F. G. Davenport, In a review in the *American Historical Review*, vol. XXII, 1906, p. 168, called these readings indispensable to the teacher.

58. Robinson and Beard, *Development of Modern Europe*, Boston, Ginn, 1907-8, 2 vols. Preface.

59. *Ibid.*, Preface.

attention to economic history, especially the industrial revolution to the influence of Beard.[60]

The success of the authors in achieving their aims appeared to be confirmed by a review written for the *History Teachers' Magazine* by Sidney B. Fay, a member of Robinson's own guild. Fay observed that from the beginning of the book the reader's eye was constantly directed to the present moment so that he might read more intelligently the dispatches of the morning paper. As to the qualities of the book, he stated: "The authors have made a textbook which is accurate, lucid, packed with information, and at the same time extremely readable. It has been used in high school and college courses and evokes real enthusiasm from students."[61]

In another review by Fay, appearing in the *American Historical Review*, he referred to *The Development of Modern Europe*, as an "adventure in the educational world" and declared that it was solid, informing, interesting, and clever. However, he could not quite reconcile himself to the extreme emphasis on the present. In questioning this practice he asked: "Is it wise, in schools and colleges, to neglect the 'cultural' value of medieval history for the practical value of some notions about contemporary Europe?"[62]

Harry Elmer Barnes in writing of this text said:

> This was an epoch-making book, in that it was the first real college textbook on modern European History published in the English language.[63] It was also the first manual on European history to

---

60. Interview with Dr. James T. Shotwell, September 5, 1945. Also see below p. 83.
61. *History Teachers' Magazine*, vol. I, 1909, p. 35.
62. *American Historical Review*, vol. XIV, 1908, p. 190.
63. Odum, *op. cit.*, pp. 389-90. It is questionable whether *The Development of Modern Europe* can be classified as the first real college text published in the English language. Myers, *The Modern Age* (Part II of his Medieval and Modern History) was published in 1903. It was an attempt to present the modern period of European history. It gave much less attention to economic, cultural, intellectual, and scientific aspects of the past. See pp. 72-74 of this work. Another history of modern Europe was Charles M. Andrews' *The Historical Development of Modern Europe*, in two volumes, 1896, and in a one volume edition in 1900 (New York, G. P. Putnams Sons). These also lacked emphasis on the non-political elements of history compared to Robinson's text. Another contemporary text was Charles Seignobos' *A Political History of Europe Since 1814*, (translated by Charles M. McVane). New York, Henry Holt, 1899; largely political as the name indicates and lacking the sweep of Robinson's text.

take into account the stupendous influence of the Industrial Revolution. . . . *The Development of Modern Europe* was, however, prepared rather hastily to meet a particular market at a given time, and was by no means the finished type of work the *History of Western Europe* exemplified.[64]

Barnes's statement to the effect that the *Development of Modern Europe* did not reach the high standard or popularity attained by *An Introduction to the History of Western Europe,* was to some degree verified by the sales of the two texts. The publishers' records show clearly that the demand for Robinson's original text was much greater than for Robinson and Beard's later one.[65]

Nevertheless, the latter text did help to set a new pattern by breaking further away from the traditional emphasis on political, institutional, and diplomatic history. This is clearly evidenced by a comparison of the *Development of Modern Europe* with two other important college texts in modern European history; namely, *The Historical Development of Modern Europe* (1900), in two volumes by Charles M. Andrews, and *A Political History of Europe Since 1814* (1899) by Charles Seignobos.[66]

Charles M. Andrews, in his *Historical Development of Modern Europe,* stated the purpose of his work as follows: "The volumes were written as an aid to a better understanding of the last eighty years of European history, and as a guide to the intricacies of the political, constitutional and diplomatic development of the leading European states during this period."[67] Andrews remained steadfast to his purpose: his text contained no treatment of the Industrial Revolution or any phases of cultural, intellectual, or scientific life.

Seignobos stated the purpose of his text a little more fully and re-

---

64. Odum, *op. cit.*, pp. 389-90.
65. Letter from Publisher, August 31, 1944.
66. Charles M. Andrews, *The Historical Development of Modern Europe from the Congress of Vienna to the Present Times,* two volumes, New York, Putnam, 1900. Charles Seignobos, *A Political History of Europe Since 1814,* (translated by Charles M. Macvane), New York, Henry Holt, 1899. Both texts were included in a select list of books recommended for a town or large school by the Committee of the New England History Teachers' Association. Special Committee of the New England History Teachers' Association, *History Syllabus for Secondary Schools,* Boston, Heath, 1904.
67. Andrews, *op. cit.*, Preface.

vealed that his primary aim was to explain the history of political evolution. He said:

> The task in hand, then, is to explain the political transformations of contemporary Europe during this period of eighty years. Being unable to deal with the whole movement of European civilization within the period, I have purposely confined myself to the political history. I have avoided all social phenomena that have had no direct effect on political life: art, science, literature, religion, private manners, and customs. I have sought chiefly to make clear the formation, composition, tactics and policies of the parties, as being the capital facts determining the fate of institutions. But I have not thought it possible to limit political history to an account of strictly political events and institutions. Aiming above all to *explain* the phenomena by showing how they are connected with each other, I have reserved room for some non-political facts: local administration, the army, the church, the schools, the press, political theories, economic systems—in all cases in which they have reacted on political life.[68]

Like Andrews, Seignobos carried out his plans as stated and gave most of his attention to political affairs. Of a total of 847 pages, he allocated eleven to a discussion of the Industrial Revolution in a chapter entitled Transformations in the Material Conditions of Life. Here Seignobos discussed some phases of the topic, such as industrial inventions, new means of destruction, use of water and steam power, new methods of communication, the growth of cities, increased wealth, and the transformation of economic life.[69] The cultural and intellectual interests and activities of man received no attention, with the exception of approximately two pages devoted to educational legislation in England, France, and Belgium.[70]

In contrast, Robinson and Beard, in their *Development of Modern Europe,* devoted one chapter of twenty-two pages to a discussion of the Industrial Revolution and the problems arising from it.[71] Probably Beard was more responsible than Robinson for the fuller treatment of the Industrial Revolution. Such responsibility is indicated by the fact

---

68. Seignobos, *op. cit.*, Preface.
69. *Ibid.*, pp. 671-682.
70. *Ibid.*, pp. 71-72, 151, 167, 145.
71. Robinson and Beard, *Development of Modern Europe*, II, pp. 30-52.

that in the two texts of which Beard and Robinson were co-authors, *The Development of Modern Europe* and the *Outlines of European History* (Part II, 1912),[72] the Industrial Revolution received relatively more attention than in either Robinson's *Introduction to the History of Western Europe* or in his *Medieval and Modern Times*.[73]

Probably even more unusual than the treatment of the Industrial Revolution was the wide variety of topics discussed in the last chapter of *The Development of Modern Europe*. The authors, while acknowledging that it was impossible to forecast the future, expressed the belief that it was reasonably clear that many problems

> now before the world are likely to engage the thoughts of intelligent and public-spirited men and women for a long time to come. Even if all of us cannot contribute directly to their solution, we should regard it as our duty to grasp the main difficulties and dangers which Europe and the world at large now face, and to follow intelligently the discussion that goes on about them. It is the purpose of this concluding chapter to suggest a few of the chief issues which will, in all probability, agitate coming generations as well as our own.[74]

This chapter of forty-eight pages, entitled Some of the Great Problems of Today, gave attention to a wide range of topics: the control of the government, what the government shall do or not do, responsible governments, women's rights, popular education, growth of a free press, relations of capital and labor, problems of the unemployed, municipal ownership, housing the poor, war on poverty, labor unions, socialism and communism, cooperatives, the class struggle, progress and effect of natural science, evolution and natural selection, atomic theory, radio-activity and medical discoveries.[75] This emphasis on modern scientific development and the political, economic and social problems of the modern age was not, however, accompanied by a discussion of the non-scientific aspects of modern culture such as art, architecture, music, literature, and the drama.

In 1908 and 1909, Robinson and Beard published two volumes of

---

72. *Ibid.* Robinson and Beard, *The Outlines of European History*, Boston, Ginn, 1912, Part II, pp. 261-282. Also see p. 80, footnote 60.
73. Robinson, *Introduction to the History of Western Europe*, pp. 675-679.
74. Robinson and Beard, *Development of Modern Europe*, II, p. 375.
75. *Ibid.*, pp. 373-421.

readings to supplement their text.[76] These were of high quality and possibly even more illuminating than those prepared to supplement the *History of Western Europe*. Sidney B. Fay, in a review of these *Readings of Modern European History,* said: "This is no mere list of unappreciated titles but an excellent critical classification which guides the student quickly to the fundamental work."[77]

In the interval between 1902 *(An Introduction to the History of Western Europe)* and 1908 *(The Development of Modern Europe)* Robinson's ideas as to aims, purposes, and organization of history had undergone an evident change. In his textbook published in 1902, Robinson had demonstrated his idea that those facts from the past should be selected which would best portray man's permanent achievements and varied activities during the intervals under consideration.[78] Robinson and Beard, in their joint publication of 1907 and 1908, demonstrated the idea that facts from the past should be definitely subordinated to the needs of the present, with the conscious aim of enabling the reader to be intelligent about his own times.

Inasmuch as this text represented the ideas of both Robinson and Beard, it is not possible to state that any specific ideas were the exclusive contribution of either author. Nevertheless, there is considerable evidence that at least three years before *The Development of Modern Europe* was published, Robinson had come to believe that it was extremely important to emphasize the modern period of history and so to present history that it should give an understanding of present-day problems. Robinson had first expressed these views in 1904 at a meeting of the Association of History Teachers of the Middle States and Maryland. At that time he complained that the high school course in medieval and modern history was unsatisfactory as it was traditionally taught, for often the student came out of the course with no greater knowledge of his own times than that of the times of Attila or Frederick Barbarossa. Of the need for emphasizing the recent period in history, Robinson said: "From the middle of the eighteenth century on, the problems loom large which still face us, and these should be allotted a more generous period in our programmes of study."[79] Thus,

---

76. James Harvey Robinson and Charles Beard, *Readings in Modern European History*, Boston, Ginn, 1908-9, 2 vols.
77. *American Historical Review*, vol. XIV, 1909, p. 639.
78. Robinson, *Introduction to the History of Western Europe*, Preface.
79. Association of History Teachers of the Middle States and Maryland, *Minutes* of the Second Annual Meeting, II, 1904, p. 36.

regardless of any influence that Beard may have exerted, it seems that Robinson himself, before the publication of the *Development of Western Europe,* in 1907-8, had become convinced of the importance of subordinating the past to the requirements of the present and of the necessity of allocating more attention to the modern period of history.

However, before a full evaluation can be made of Robinson's contributions to the teaching of history through his texts, it will be necessary to examine his later texts and the various revisions of his earlier ones to determine whether they continued to maintain the educational leadership offered by his influential book, *An Introduction to the History of Western Europe.*

In 1918 Robinson prepared a seventy-four page supplement, *The Last Decade of European History and the Great War,*[80] designed to supplement both the *Introduction to the History of Western Europe* and the *Development of Modern Europe.* The supplement could be purchased separately for those who had the first editions of those earlier texts. The 1918 edition of the *Introduction to the History of Western Europe* had the supplement bound with the text. The supplement followed the bibliography and index of the volume and appeared much like a postscript. In other respects the 1902-3 edition and the 1918 edition of the *Introduction to the History of Western Europe* were identical.[81] Apparently neither Robinson nor his publishers felt that a discussion of the Great War demanded rewriting or refocusing of any chapters that dealt with the history preceding 1914. The students who were using the *Development of Modern Europe,* 1907-8, had to purchase their supplement separately, for no revision was made in this text until 1929-30.

The first text to undergo thorough revision was his influential two-volume work, *Introduction to the History of Western Europe,* originally published in 1902-3. The first major revision made by Robinson was in 1924-26; the second (and last) was in 1934.[82]

Robinson's increased interest in and preoccupation with the function and purpose of history, the possibility of utilizing history for social

---

80. J. H. Robinson, *The Last Decade of European History and the Great War,* Designed as a supplement to *The Development of Modern Europe* and the *Introduction to the History of Western Europe,* Boston, Ginn, 1918.

81. Robinson, *Introduction to the History of Western Europe,* Boston, Ginn, 1918.

82. Dr. James T. Shotwell is now working on a revision of the 1934 edition. Interview with Dr. Shotwell, September 5, 1945.

betterment, as he expressed it in *The New History* and in his later university classes, were equally apparent in the later editions of his college texts. His 1902-3 edition contained only an eight-page chapter on The Historical Point of View, whereas his later editions expanded it to sixteen pages.[83]

In the first edition, published at the turn of the century, his object was to explain the most significant achievements of Western civilization. However, in his later editions, this aim is broadened to include another objective:

> There are many persistent mistakes and prejudices which run counter to our new knowledge and conditions and possibilities. It is difficult for us to make adjustments to novel situations, for we always have to be taking account of historical habits formed long ago in the Middle Ages or earlier. So the study of history should make a great contribution to better understanding of life and to the formation of more thoughtful opinions on public affairs.[84]

Here Robinson expressed the feeling that the past is not only living but that it also offers a golden key to the understanding of things as they are. This key, when properly used, would reveal to us that, although all progress must necessarily be based upon the past, the past was always holding us back. Therefore, the author warned his readers, the past became at once an indispensable support and counsellor, and at the same time a subtle enemy of proper adjustments and accommodations to ever new conditions and increasing knowledge.[85]

Hence, the contrast of the aims expressed in the first edition of his text with those of two and three decades later discloses that his later texts quite clearly reflect his growing interest in social betterment and his determination that history should contribute to that goal.

In addition to a restatement of aims, the 1924-6 edition gave much more space to the modern aspects of European history. There were new chapters: Great Britain and her Empire, World Trade and Imperialism, Russia and the Near East, The World War, Europe Since the War, and International Relations.[86] The addition of these, of course,

---

83. Robinson, *An Introduction to the History of Western Europe*, I, 1924; also I, 1934. These editions were exactly alike in this feature, and they have the same preface.
84. *Ibid.*, II, 1934 edition is the same.
85. *Ibid.*, I, p. 3. The 1924- and 1934 editions are the same.
86. *Ibid.*, Table of Contents.

was manifestly to bring the text up to date. However, the unique feature of this text was the addition of two new chapters entitled New Conceptions of the World We Live In and New Views of Man's Nature and Traditions. These chapters, as their titles indicated, were devoted to a phase of intellectual history. His increased attention to intellectual history—manifested in these two chapters—confined itself to a discussion of the newer discoveries in modern science and their possible implication for man.[87] Robinson still totally ignored other phases of intellectual development, such as the literature, music, art, and architecture of our modern age.[88] His greater interest in the scientific phase of modern intellectual and cultural history became apparent; four pages dealt with this problem in his first edition, but fifty-three pages were allocated to the same phase in his later editions.[89]

In his consideration of the intellectual and cultural aspects of the Middle Ages and the Renaissance, there is little difference, however, between the earlier and later editions. These phases of the past, which he had handled so well in his text of 1902-3, were carried over with little change into the newer editions.[90] Interestingly enough, in treating the cultural and intellectual aspects of the Middle Ages, Robinson included a discussion of language, literature, science, philosophy and art; in treating the cultural and intellectual aspects of the modern age he ignored almost all achievements except those of scientific progress.[91]

Another innovation in his later editions was his assignment of an entire chapter to the discussion of plans for bettering human relations including the doctrines of Fourier, Robert Owen, the English Fabians, and Karl Marx. In the 1924-26 edition he expanded his discussion of social theory and progress to a twenty-six page chapter, and in his 1934 edition to a forty-page chapter.[92] In his first edition the only indication of interest in this phase of the past was included in

---

87. *Ibid.*, II, pp. 505-558, 1924 edition.
88. *Ibid.*
89. *Ibid.*, II, pp. 505-558 (1924-26 and 1934 editions); pp. 671-675 in 1902-3 edition.
90. The material was rearranged to some extent, but basically it was the same. However, the later edition contained about three pages more on these phases than the 1902-3 edition. Robinson, *Introduction to the History of Western Europe*, I, of 1902-3 and 1924-26 and 1934 editions.
91. *Ibid.*, 1902-3 edition, pp. 250-276 and pp. 321-353; all other editions pp. 278-340.
92. *Ibid.*, pp. 559-585 (1924-26 edition); pp. 559-599 (1934 edition).

about a page in which he briefly discussed government regulations protecting labor.[93]

Oddly enough, this heightened interest in the new science and an interest to a lesser degree in the theories of social betterment were not paralleled by a greater emphasis on the economic phases of our past and present. The Industrial Revolution, which he frequently admitted was one of the innovations of our age, was definitely slighted. The author did not consider it significant enough to devote a separate chapter to it; whatever material there was on this subject was scattered throughout the next and subordinated to other subjects. For instance, the Industrial Revolution received a total of seven pages; six were in a chapter entitled Great Britain and her Empire; the remaining page was tucked in a chapter called Russia and the Near-Eastern Question.[94]

The shift of emphasis which was revealed in Robinson's *Introduction to the History of Western Europe* was equally manifest in his revised edition of the *Development of Modern Europe*[95] which, in collaboration with Beard, was first published in 1907-8 and revised in 1929-30. Here again, in 1929, in stating his concept of history, Robinson reiterated that history must be made to serve our present needs, and that past events as such were not necessarily worth recalling.[96] Two of the chapters on intellectual and cultural history appearing in this revised edition of the *Development of Modern Europe* were taken almost intact from the 1924-26 edition of *An Introduction to the History of Western Europe*.[97] However, in volume two of the text in modern history, the authors made an important addition of intellectual and cultural material by adding a twenty-five page chapter entitled *The Study of Mankind in Fiction*. Nevertheless, as important as this

93. *Ibid.*, pp. 681, 1902-3 edition.
94. *Ibid.*, pp. 368-374 and 423-24. This is the same in both 1924-26 and 1934 editions.
95. Robinson and Beard, *The Development of Modern Europe*, Boston, Ginn, 2 vols., 1924-26.
96. *Ibid.*, I, 1. Here again eight pages are devoted to explaining the plans and aims of the book.
97. Robinson, *An Introduction to the History of Western Europe*, II, 1926. Table of Contents; also Robinson and Beard, *Development of Modern Europe*, II, 1930, Table of Contents. The two chapters appeared in both texts and were entitled New Conceptions of the World in Which We Live and New Views of Man's Nature and Tradition. The chapter entitled The Study of Mankind in Fiction reflected Robinson's interest in the value of the modern drama and novel as an historical source at this time. See Robinson, "The New Ways of Historians" *American Historical Review*, vol. XXXV, pp. 254-255.

innovation was, Robinson and Beard still omitted discussions of other phases of our cultural life such as music, art, and architecture.

In the *Development of Modern Europe*, the Industrial Revolution received about the same type of treatment or lack of treatment as in the revised edition of *An Introduction to the History of Western Europe*. The authors did not devote any single chapter to this important phase of the past and present, but brought it in fragmentarily in connection with other topics.[98] This arrangement failed to emphasize this movement in proportion to its importance in explaining much of modern life and problems. In contrast other college textbooks, especially those of Robinson's former students, Carlton J. H. Hayes and J. Salwyn Schapiro which were apparently superseding those of Robinson by this time, were devoting much more attention to the industrial revolution and the economic and social problems created by it.[99]

TEXTS FOR SECONDARY SCHOOLS

In the publications of which he was sole or joint author, *An Introduction to the History of Western Europe* (1902), *Readings in European History* (1904-6), *Development of Modern Europe* (1907-8), *Readings in Modern European History* (1908), Robinson had been aiming at students in college and readers of that capacity. In 1912, he turned his attention to secondary school students.

His first enterprise in this field was in collaboration with James Henry Breasted, professor of Egyptology and Oriental History in the University of Chicago. Their text consisted of two volumes providing a general survey of history from the earliest times down to 1914. It bore the title, *Outlines of European History:* Part I, *Earliest Man to the Opening of the Eighteenth Century;* Part II, *From the Seventeenth Century to the Present Time.*[100]

In the first volume, Breasted assumed responsibility for the material

---

98. Robinson and Beard, *The Development of Modern Europe*, I, II, Table of Contents.
99. Carlton J. H. Hayes, *A Political and Social History of Modern Europe*, New York, Macmillan, 1928, 2 vols. see vol. II, pp. 67-97 and J. Salwyn Schapiro, *Modern Contemporary European History*, New York, Houghton Mifflin, 1931. See pp. 20-48 and pp. 540-559.
100. James H. Breasted, *Outlines of European History*: Part I, *Earliest Man The Orient, Greece and Rome*, 1914. James H. Robinson and Charles A. Beard, *Outlines of European History*: Part II, *From the Opening of the Eighteenth Century to the Present Day*, 1912.

dealing with the ages from earliest man to approximately the breakup of the Roman Empire.[101] At this point Robinson took over and continued the volume through the reign of Louis XIV. The second volume was the joint work of Robinson and Charles A. Beard, and covered European history from the opening of the eighteenth century to the year of publication.

Robinson, in preparing his share of Part I, according to his own words, freely used "corresponding matter" from his *Introduction to the History of Western Europe*.[102] In the preface to Part II of the *Outlines of European History,* Robinson and Beard wrote: "The present volume is in the main a condensation and revision of the authors' large work, *The Development of Modern Europe,* which has been brought down to date by a review of the last decade of European policies."[103] An examination of Part II, *Outlines of European History,* causes doubt whether the authors had faith in their own innovations of 1907-8. Their "condensation and revision" of the *Development of Modern Europe* quite naturally required that some material be omitted, so the omission was made. However, the authors chose to omit one of the unique features of the earlier work; namely, the last chapter, in which they had devoted forty-eight pages to a discussion of some important contemporary problems. This chapter, in the original college edition, was a vital discussion of such topics as science and its tremendous influence, popular education, housing, and socialism.[104] All these were omitted from the high school text; in their place was a chapter entitled The Last Decade of European Politics, consisting of twenty-eight pages: sixteen on social and political reform in England, Germany, Portugal, Turkey, China, and Russia; two and one-half pages on woman suffrage; and the last twelve pages on social reform.[105] Never was there any mention of modern science or other phases of intellectual or cultural history. Thus it would appear that the authors, who were willing to make and who had made innovations in their college texts, were still thinking in traditional terms as far as the secondary-school level was concerned.

101. Robinson and Breasted, *Outlines of European History*, I, Preface.
102. *Ibid.*, Preface. Part II was first published in 1912 and Part I in 1916.
103. Robinson and Breasted, *Outlines of European History*, II, Preface. In the preface the authors also reiterate their belief that history should explain the present.
104. Robinson and Beard, *Development of Modern Europe*, II, pp. 373-521.
105. Robinson and Breasted, *Outlines of European History*, II, pp. 506-534.

P. W. Shortridge, in a review appearing in the *History Teachers' Magazine,* asserted that Volume II was really a college text made smaller, and that the authors had found it more expedient to omit rather than to explain in simpler form. The reviewer further observed that the language and vocabulary were about the same as in the original college edition.[106]

This attempt of Robinson and Beard to make their secondary-school text simpler and smaller by the mere process of omission rendered the book less comprehensible to the high school student. This fact appeared especially striking upon comparison of the treatment given the Industrial Revolution in the earlier college text, the *Development of Modern Europe* (1907-08) with the later treatment appearing in the *Outlines of European History,* Part II. In the college text Robinson and Beard explained in great detail the processes of spinning and weaving in early times and the revolutionizing of these processes by the inventions of the eighteenth century. The authors' simple, lucid descriptions were accompanied by pictures and diagrams to make the whole account more meaningful. Likewise their explanations of the invention of the steam engine, accompanied by pictures and diagrams, was detailed enough to be expressive. The authors followed their account of the various early inventions with a discussion of the social and economic implications of the Industrial Revolution.[107]

However, in the *Outlines of European History,* Part II, the authors gave no such eloquent explanation of the beginnings of the Industrial Revolution. There was not a single drawing of a machine old or new. Instead, the student was presented with generalizations on the beginning of the Industrial Revolution and on the great changes brought on by the new machines. Yet the high school text gave serious consideration to Fourier, Karl Marx, the class struggle, and the theory of individualism, all of which had been omitted in the earlier college texts.[108] It would seem that the *Outlines of European History,* II, was not only a college text made smaller but also less interesting and less comprehensible.

In spite of these shortcomings, the authors asserted that their texts

---

106. *The History Teachers' Magazine,* vol., III, 1913, p. 270.
107. Robinson and Beard, *The Development of Modern Europe,* vol. II, 1908, pp. 30-52.
108. Robinson and Breasted, *Outlines of European History,* vol. II, pp. 261-282.

were innovations in that they met a growing demand in the high school for a two-year course in European history.[109] There were some indications that this was true. The Committee on the Social Studies in Secondary Education, reporting in 1916, did not recommend that English history and medieval history as courses be continued in the secondary-school curriculum; rather they proposed that two years be given to the study of European History. Thus it would appear that the *Outlines of European History,* appearing in 1912 and 1916, anticipated the newly proposed two-year course in European history and the resultant demand for textual material.

Robinson's later secondary-school texts were written for three different, though overlapping, courses in European history; namely, Medieval and Modern History, World History, and Modern European History. A comparison of his texts in each of these fields with at least two contemporary texts of the same scope and general content aids in evaluating Robinson's influence on the teaching of history in the secondary schools.

Robinson's second high school textbook was his *Medieval and Modern Times,* published originally in 1916 and revised in 1919.[110] This volume, the author tells us, was a careful, thoroughgoing revision of the *Introduction to the History of Western Europe,* which first appeared in 1902-3. Robinson stated that the presentation had been simplified so as to adapt the book to the secondary level; also, the treatment of medieval times had been reduced so that attention could be given to the developments of the past one hundred years.[111]

Other volumes of the same scope and same general purpose as Robinson's were *Medieval and Modern History* by Hutton Webster (1919), and *Medieval and Modern History* by Philip Van Ness Myers (1920).[112] Both Myers and Webster, in their prefaces, echoed Robinson's earlier proposals for reorganizing European history. Myers explained that his account of the medieval period had been compressed

---

109. *Ibid.,* I, Preface.
110. Robinson, *Medieval and Modern Times,* Boston, Ginn, 1916 and 1919. The 1919 edition will be used here for comparative purposes as it corresponds more closely to the date of publication of the two other texts with which it will be compared.
111. *Ibid.,* Preface.
112. Hutton Webster, *Medieval and Modern History,* New York, D. C. Heath, 1919, pp. 743. Philip Van Ness Myers, *Medieval and Modern History,* Boston, Ginn, 1920, pp. 672.

to make possible more attention to later history.[113] Webster allied himself even further to Robinson by stating that the prime business of an author of a textbook in this field was to clarify the remote and the immediate causes of the great challenges of the present times.[114]

In a comparison of these texts by Robinson, Myers, and Webster, attention will fall particularly on their treatment and emphasis of the following aspects of medieval and modern history: medieval church, medieval civilization, the Renaissance, geographic discoveries, commercial expansion, the French Revolution, the Industrial Revolution, and social and intellectual aspects of modern life.

Robinson gave more attention to the medieval church than did either of the other authors. He devoted fifty-two pages to a discussion of the medieval church up to the Reformation; Myers and Webster devoted thirty-six and thirty-seven pages respectively.[115] Robinson's detailed, comprehensive treatment of this subject was to be expected as a result of his extensive treatment of that subject in his *Introduction to the History of Western Europe,* published in 1902-3. Considering the wide range of material to be covered, both Myers and Webster also gave a satisfactory treatment of the subject. In portraying various phases of medieval civilization, such as science, books, town life, and the general social and intellectual life of the period, other than religious, Webster devoted a total of seventy-four pages to a well-rounded discussion of these phases of the past as against Robinson's sixty-two pages and Myer's fifty. Although Robinson had led in breaking away from political and military history in the early part of the century and had insistently pleaded for a broadened view of the past, it is noteworthy that he did not maintain this leadership in portraying the intellectual and cultural aspects of the past in his medieval and modern history textbook on the secondary-level.

In the consideration given to geographic discoveries and commercial expansion, Webster gave over to these topics a total of sixty-five pages; Robinson slighted this subject with a mere seventeen pages in one chapter, to which he gave the title How England Became Queen of the Ocean. (Robinson, in this topic, had transplanted word for word whole

---

113. Myers, *Medieval and Modern History,* Preface.
114. H. Webster, *Medieval and Modern History,* Preface.
115. Robinson, *Medieval and Modern Times* (1919), pp. 40-54, 54-64, 144-158, 181-195. Myers, *Medieval and Modern History* (1920), pp. 14-28, 103-110, 134-149. Webster, *Medieval and Modern History,* (1919), pp. 45-60, 137-159.

sentences and paragraphs from his 1902-3 edition of his *Introduction to the History of Western Europe*.)[116] Myer's text, with only nineteen pages on this topic, seemed to be as much bound by tradition as Robinson's.

In treating the French Revolution and the Napoleonic Era, Robinson went into much more detail than did either Myers or Webster. Robinson devoted 101 pages to a discussion of this phase of the past, while Myers totaled sixty-seven, and Webster, sixty-one.[117] However, the real difference in the history texts can not be measured by counting the number of pages devoted to the French Revolution and Napoleonic Era, but by a comparison of the emphasis given various phases of the subject. The first notable difference in emphasis occurred in the treatment of the background of the French Revolution up to the Call of the Estates General in 1789. Both Robinson and Webster allocated about one-third of their total account of the French Revolution and Napoleonic Era to this phase of the subject; Myers devoted only one-fifth of his discussion to this aspect.[118] A further comparison of the three texts reveals many differences in the treatment of two other aspects of the Revolution: namely, the period from 1789 to 1799 and the Reign of Terror. In discussing the French Revolution from 1789 to 1799—that is, between the Tennis Court Oath and the rise of Napoleon as First Consul,—Robinson devoted thirty-six pages, Myers twenty-seven, and Webster nineteen.[119] The Reign of Terror received eight pages from Robinson, six from Myers, and approximately one

---

116. In *Medieval and Modern Times* the chapter is entitled How England Became Queen of the Ocean; in *Introduction to the History of Western Europe*, 1902-3, it is called The Expansion of England. There is a slight rearrangement of material and a little added and a little omitted.

117. Robinson, *Medieval and Modern Times* (1919), pp. 461-562. Myers, *Medieval and Modern History* (1920), pp. 437-504. Webster, *Medieval and Modern History* (1919), pp. 480-541.

118. Robinson, *Medieval and Modern Times* (1919), pp. 461-491. Myers, *Medieval and Modern History* (1920), pp. 437-450. Webster, *Medieval and Modern History* (1919), pp. 480-501. As background for the French Revolution, Robinson had two chapters entitled Modern Science and the Spirit of Reform and The Eve of the French Revolution; Webster had one chapter entitled the Old Régime in Europe. Additional background on the French Revolution was also in the chapter entitled The Revolutionary and Napoleonic Era.

119. Robinson, *Medieval and Modern Times* (1919), pp. 497-533. Myers, *Medieval and Modern History* (1920), pp. 448-475. Webster, *Medieval and Modern History* (1919), pp. 503-522.

and one-half from Webster.[120] Robinson's large number of pages were accounted for by his increased attention to details, not only those required to give a full account of the events and conditions leading to the Revolution, but also to those details which, at one time, he himself had suggested were relatively unimportant.[121] On the other hand Myers apparently followed his traditional pattern of including a wide range of details with no special emphasis on any point.[122] Webster, however, while giving proportionally as much attention to a discussion of the backgrounds of the French Revolution as Robinson, omitted many of the details of the events from 1789 to 1799, especially those of the Reign of Terror. Some of the space thus saved by Webster was devoted to a more comprehensive discussion of the Industrial Revolution and to man's cultural and intellectual achievements.

The treatments accorded the Industrial Revolution in the medieval and modern history texts of Robinson, Myers, and Webster were also considerably different in emphasis. Myers dismissed the subject with a chapter of only five pages entitled *The New Industrialism*.[123] Robinson devoted a chapter of fourteen pages to this topic,[124] nearly three times the number of pages by Myers, but one-third less in number than those by Robinson and Beard in *The Outlines of European History* Part II, 1912.[125] Robinson, in preparing this brief fourteen-page chapter on the Industrial Revolution, drew heavily from the materials appearing in the text previously prepared by Beard and himself. In fact, a comparison of the material in the chapter on the Industrial Revolution first appearing in Robinson and Beard's *Development of Modern Europe* (1907-8) with the treatment of this subject in the *Outlines of European History*, Part II (1912) by the same authors, and with the treatment in Robinson's *Medieval and Modern Times* (1919) disclosed whole paragraphs and even pages identical in every respect.[126] Robinson, in treating this

120. Robinson, *Medieval and Modern Times* (1919), pp. 516-524. Myers, *Medieval and Modern History* (1920), pp. 463-569; Webster, *Medieval and Modern History* (1919), pp. 518-19.
121. Robinson, "The Teaching of European History in College" American Historical Association, *Annual Report*, 1896, vol., I, pp. 271-6.
122. See page 73.
123. Myers, *Medieval and Modern History* (1920), pp. 579-84.
124. Robinson, *Medieval and Modern Times* (1919), pp. 580-594.
125. Robinson and Beard, *Outlines of European History*, II, pp. 261-282.
126. Robinson and Beard, *Development of Modern Europe* II, pp. 30-52. Robinson and Beard, *Outlines of European History* II, pp. 261-282. Robinson, *Medieval and Modern Times*, pp. 580-94.

significant phase of man's development, was seemingly averse to proceeding on new lines, preferring to rely on selections from material prepared for earlier texts by Beard and himself.

Of course, Robinson's treatment appeared quite complete when compared to the five pages on this subject by Myers. However, in Webster's *Medieval and Modern History* (1919), the author went far beyond Robinson, with a well rounded thirty-four page discussion of the past and present significance of the Revolution.[127] Robinson's lack of emphasis on this phase of history was the more significant in that it was he who had so often insisted that the historian should largely concern himself with the major achievements of man.

Lastly, in the amount of material on cultural and intellectual history during the nineteenth century, as given by the three authors in their respective texts, Robinson, the pioneer in this field at the turn of the century, no longer maintained leadership. Neither Robinson in his *Medieval and Modern Times* (1919), nor Myers in his *Medieval and Modern History* (1920), devoted a single page to these aspects of man's development.[128] This is in contrast to Robinson's earlier emphasis on this field in his *Introduction to the History of Western Europe,* 1902-3, in which he had allocated a seventeen-page chapter to a discussion of cultural, economic, scientific, and social advance, and to the later emphasis by Beard and himself in their *Development of Modern Europe,* 1907-8, in which there was a forty-eight page discussion.[129] Webster was the only one of the three authors who dealt with the subject. In one well-written and pictorially illustrated chapter of thirty-two pages entitled Modern Civilization, Webster dealt with a variety of human interests and activities; such as modern science, emancipation of women and children, separation of church and state, popular education, higher learning, music, literature, fine arts, and other subjects of a similar nature. This chapter also discusses the contributions of outstanding leaders in various fields of human endeavor such as John Wesley, Marie Curie, Herbert Spencer, Sir Walter Scott, Charles Dickens, Victor Hugo, Richard Wagner, and Ludwig Beethoven.[130]

127. Webster, *Medieval and Modern History*, pp. 640-74.
128. Robinson, *Medieval and Modern Times*, 1919. Myers, *Medieval and Modern History*, 1920.
129. Robinson, *Introduction to the History of Western Europe*, 1902-3, pp. 670-687. Robinson and Beard, *The Development of Modern Europe*, 1907-8, II, pp. 373-421.
130. Webster, *Medieval and Modern History*, pp. 675-707.

TEACHER OF HISTORY

Robinson's high school text in the field of medieval and modern history apparently no longer offered to students the broader concepts of the past, which he had so ably championed in his early college texts. His lack of interest in the economic phases of the past, especially in those of the Industrial Revolution, and his neglect of the broader phases of our modern cultural and intellectual life, resulted in the loss of his pioneer leadership in portraying the varied interests and activities of man.

Robinson's next text, one in the field of world history, followed the pattern of his earlier texts in many ways. This book, titled *A General History of Europe*,[131] was written in collaboration with James Henry Breasted and Emma Peters Smith. It was an adaptation and abridgment of the *Outlines of European History*, Parts I and II, published by Robinson, Breasted, and Beard in 1912-16.[132]

This *General History of Europe* was comparable to three contemporary texts of about the same scope and organization: Henry Elson's *Modern Times and the Living Past* (1921), Willis M. West's *The Story of World Progress* (1922), and Hutton Webster's *World History* (1919).[133]

Robinson, in *A General History of Europe*, as in *Medieval and Modern Times*, gave little attention to the Industrial Revolution. Both he and Elson devoted one chapter of eleven pages to such a discussion; West, fourteen pages; but Webster, a forty-two page chapter, comparable to his similar discussion in *Medieval and Modern History*.[134]

However, the cultural and intellectual life during the Middle Ages and the Renaissance was emphasized in Robinson's textbook; for he wrote twenty-eight pages on this subject. Webster, Elson, and West wrote seventeen, fifteen, and ten respectively.[135] Robinson's fuller treat-

131. Robinson, Breasted, and Smith, *A General History of Europe*, Boston, Ginn, 1921. In 1924 the title was changed to *Our World Today and Yesterday*.
132. Robinson, Breasted and Beard, *Outlines of European History*, Parts I, and II, Boston, Ginn, 1912-16. See p. 95, footnote 126.
133. Henry W. Elson, *Modern Times and the Living Past*, New York, American Book, 1921. Hutton Webster, *World History*, New York, Heath, 1921. Willis M. West, *The Story of World Progress*, New York, Allyn and Bacon, 1922.
134. Robinson, Breasted and Smith, *A General History of Europe*, pp. 487-498. Elson, *Modern Times and the Living Past*, pp. 502-13. West, *The Story of World Progress*, pp. 465-79. Webster, *World History*, pp. 481-523.
135. Robinson, Breasted and Smith, *A General History of Europe*, pp. 264-278, 289-299. Elson, *Modern Times and the Living Past*, pp. 300-315. West,

ment of the question may be explained by his earlier interest in this aspect of history and perhaps by the fact that the authors found it comparatively easy to turn to the *Outlines of European History,* Part I, which Robinson and Breasted had published in 1916, and to use whole paragraphs and even pages from its chapter on Books and Science during the Middle Ages.[136] In preparing this particular material for their *General European History,* the authors reorganized part of the original chapter of the earlier text and added some illustrations; nevertheless, the relationship is unmistakable.

Robinson did not retain this emphasis on the cultural and intellectual activities in his discussion of the modern period. Webster's discussion, once again, was fuller. Although Robinson's attention to this subject was considerably greater than that of either Elson or West, Webster's discussion was more than twice as long as Robinson's.[137]

Next, in one other field of secondary-school history, that of modern European, Robinson, in collaboration with Charles A. Beard, produced a text. The first edition of their text in this field appeared in 1921 and was called a *History of Europe: Our Own Times.*[138] A revised edition was published in 1934.

An evaluation of this edition, one of his most important later texts, is possible by choosing two contemporary texts in the same area for comparative purposes: Carl Becker's *Modern History,* and Hutton Webster's *Modern European Civilization,* both published in 1933.[139]

All three of these texts included a chapter on the Industrial Revolution, but the chapter in Robinson and Beard's volume contained approximately one-half the number of pages of either of the other texts.[140]

The Story of World Progress, pp. 301-4, 321-7, 357-8. Webster, *World History,* pp. 231-248.

136. Compare Robinson, Breasted and Beard, *A General History of Europe,* pp. 264-278, and Robinson & Breasted, *Outlines of European History,* Part I, 1912, pp. 533-60.

137. Robinson, Breasted and Smith, *A General History of Europe,* pp. 589-599. Elson, *Modern Times and the Living Past,* pp. 642-645. West, *The Story of World Progress,* pp. 595-8. Webster, *World History,* pp. 625-49.

138. Robinson and Beard, *History of Europe; Our Own Times,* Boston, Ginn, 1934.

139. Carl Becker, *Modern History,* New York, Silver, Burdett, 1933, p. 821. Becker was a student of Robinson's in the early part of this century. Webster, *Modern European Civilization,* New York, Heath, 1933, p. 761.

140. Robinson's text had one chapter of 12 pages; Becker's one chapter of 25 pages; Webster's one chapter of 22 pages. See their respective texts.

This does not tell the whole story, for both Becker and Webster followed their chapter on the Industrial Revolution with another chapter describing its effect on man and his manner of living.[141] Robinson and Beard included nothing of this, except selections two or three pages in length scattered throughout the text.[142]

The treatment given modern cultural and intellectual history indicated again that Robinson no longer retained leadership in this field in which he had once been so influential. Robinson and Beard devoted one chapter of sixteen pages to a discussion of modern knowledge and invention, treating the subject in their traditional manner. Their chapter, entitled Progress of Modern Knowledge and Invention, devoted thirteen pages to a discussion of modern science, and three pages to a discussion of the "new history" and democratization of knowledge.[143] However, Robinson and Beard, even in treating this subject in such a manner, did more than Becker, who offered no separate discussion of this phase of man's development. Instead, whatever Becker had to say on the newer scientific discoveries and inventions appeared in his earlier chapters on the Industrial Revolution.[144] Likewise, he omitted all mention of art, architecture, music, literature, education, and the other aspects of cultural and intellectual history.[145] Webster expanded his treatment of this subject into a thirty-four page chapter called Intellectual Enlightenment, in which he described a variety of topics; modern and applied science, philosophy, and the social studies, literature, music, other fine arts, and cosmopolitanism.[146]

Study of the range of Robinson's secondary-school texts in history demonstrates that for the most part his texts tended to follow the same pattern and emphasis laid down in the first editions of his *Introduction to the History of Western Europe* and his *Development of Modern*

---

141. Becker, *Modern History*, pp. 526-547. How the Industrial Revolution Gave Rise to Modern Socialism and the Conflict over Social Reform. Webster, *Modern European Civilization*, pp. 270-294. Outcome of the Industrial Revolution.
142. Robinson, and Beard, *History of Europe: Our Own Times*, pp. 416-418, 471-475.
143. Robinson and Beard, *History of Europe: Our Own Times*, pp. 500-517.
144. Becker, *Modern History*, pp. 499-547.
145. This refers to the modern aspects of cultural and intellectual history and does not refer to the revolutionary ideas which helped to prepare for the French Revolution. To the History of Thought just preceding the French Revolution, Becker gives 35 pages, Robinson and Beard 17 pages, Webster 14 pages.
146. Webster, *Modern European Civilization*, pp. 576-610.

Europe. His efforts to reduce the size of his text for secondary-school use often led him, however, to omit many enriching details and some of the more important phases of cultural and intellectual history, in which he had pioneered. The texts in which he collaborated with Beard contained a larger treatment of the Industrial Revolution than those which he wrote alone.

Hence Robinson, by restricting himself to the pattern of history appearing in his earlier college texts which gave relatively little attention to the non-scientific phases of modern cultural and intellectual history and modern economic history, was, by the second decade of this century, outdistanced by other authors of history texts who were not bound by their own tradition and were eager to portray all aspects of man's past.

Thus it would appear that Robinson had only limited success in placing his concepts of the new history in his history texts. Robinson through his neglect of economic history, especially the industrial revolution and the numerous social and economic problems stemming from it, and through his neglect of the non-scientific aspects of modern cultural and intellectual history failed to give his history the comprehensiveness which he had earlier demanded of the "new history." Moreover by failing to treat adequately the economic history of the past two centuries he had neglected to a large degree to explain the basis and origin of many of the social, economic, political, and educational problems of our own age; a requirement which Robinson had claimed to be an essential step in securing social progress and human betterment, the major goals of our time.

Nevertheless, although Robinson's text failed to achieve completely the high aspirations proclaimed in the *New History,* his early college texts *An Introduction to the History of Western Europe* (1902-3) and, in collaboration with Beard, the *Development of Modern Europe* (1907-8), did start a trend which seems to have been generally followed by later writers of European history texts. The authors of European history texts that followed Robinson accepted as their aims and purposes and attempted to carry out, with varying degrees of success, three important principles established by Robinson: history should attempt to reveal the manifold activities of man, not merely the political, diplomatic, and military affairs; more emphasis should be placed upon the recent period of history; lastly, history should contribute to an understanding and, if possible, a solution of some of our present day problems.

4

Robinson's Influences

PERHAPS one of Robinson's most direct influences on the teaching of history in colleges and universities was exerted through the publication of his college textbooks in the field of European history. As has been previously indicated, his most famous enterprise in this field was *An Introduction to the History of Western Europe* (1902-3), which set a new standard for the writing of textbooks on European history in this country.¹ Speaking from the point of view of a college professor of history J. Salwyn Schapiro, wrote:

> Robinson's chief title to fame ... was as the author of the textbooks on European history. In 1903 appeared a volume from his pen entitled *History of Western Europe* which dealt with the medieval and modern periods. Literally it marked a revolution in the teaching of history in the high school and college. The pre-Robinson textbooks were, as a rule, dry outlines of political and military events, generally products of hack writers or tired historians. Robinson's history was a solid book of scholarship, written in a delightful style, and included social and cultural materials that were then novel in history manuals. It was also distinctly liberal and progressive in tone. The volume went through many editions and literally swept the country. It became the inspiration of a new school of writers of textbooks of European history that have since carried the subject far beyond Robinson's initial inspiration. The students throughout the land who now read their textbooks of European history with delight and whose feet are set in the path of progress may well be grateful to James Harvey Robinson.²

Professor Lynn Thorndike, another of Robinson's earlier students, reinforced Schapiro's statement as to the significance for the teaching of history in colleges of Robinson's famous text: *"An Introduction to the History of Western Europe* ... having been studied by youth whose

---

1. Barnes, *loc. cit.*, p. 389.
2. J. Salwyn Schapiro, "James Harvey Robinson (1863-1936)." *Journal of Social Philosophy* vol. I, 1936, p. 281.

minds were still in a plastic state, has undoubtedly exerted a much greater, deeper, and more lasting impression upon human thought than any of his volumes intended for 'the trade' and general reading public."[3]

A further indication of the wide influence in colleges of this famous history textbook is revealed by the large number of copies sold during the first quarter of this century. Barnes stated that the first edition (1902-1924) sold 250,000 copies.[4] These figures are, to a large degree, supported by the publisher who, though unwilling to make public the details of publication or sales figures, stated that "thirty years ago it was selling at the rate of from ten to thirty thousand copies per year."[5] In addition to its wide appeal in the United States, volume one of the 1924 edition was translated into Chinese and in 1929 into Urdu.[6]

Robinson's accompanying *Readings in European History* were also well received. Between 1914 and 1944 over 36,000 copies of volume one and over 31,000 copies of volume two were sold. This was in addition to 22,000 copies sold in the one-volume abridged edition.[7]

In the University of Missouri, *An Introduction to the History of Western Europe* served not only as the text for the course in European history but also as the basis for a syllabus written by Professor Norman Maclaren Trenholme. This syllabus, totalling 194 pages, consisted of Part I, *The Middle Ages,* and Part II, *The Modern Age.* The author, in speaking of his reliance upon Robinson's *Introduction to the History of Western Europe* said, "The author intends his syllabus to be an aid to the study of *History of Western Europe* and the *Readings in European History*."[8]

Robinson's text was of course, used in many other colleges. The Dartmouth history department's *Syllabus in Modern European History* (1920-21) listed four textbooks as required reading: *An Introduction*

---

3. Lynn Thorndike, "A Review of the Human Comedy by James Harvey Robinson (1937)", *Journal of Modern History*, vol. IX, September 1937, pp. 367-8. The volumes intended for "the trade" refers to *The Mind in the Making* and *The Humanizing of Knowledge*.

4. Odum, *op. cit.*, p. 388.

5. Letter from publisher, May 28, 1945.

6. Bibliography of James Harvey Robinson reprinted from *A Bibliography of the Faculty of Political Science, 1880-1930*, Columbia University Press, 1931.

7. Letter from publisher, August 31, 1944. These figures go back only thirty years.

8. Norman Maclaren Trenholme, *A Syllabus for the History of Western Europe*, Boston, Ginn, 1907.

to the *History of Western Europe*[9] and three others. This syllabus, first published in 1910, went through eight editions by 1921. There is no record of how long after 1921 it was used. In the College of the City of New York, Robinson's textbook in European History served for nearly a decade as a basic text for courses in medieval and modern history.[10]

Although his other college textbook in European history, *The Development of Modern Europe,* which was done in collaboration with Charles A. Beard, did not receive so great a reception as Robinson's original text, the publishers have indicated that the sales were considerable. From 1914 to 1944 over 56,000 copies of volume one and over 54,000 copies of volume two were sold.[11] These figures do not give the complete picture in as much as the sales from 1907 (when it was first published) to 1914 were not given. The sales for this period were undoubtedly quite large as this textbook contained many innovations not included in contemporaneous volumes.[12] Moreover, this was before Carlton J. H. Hayes and J. Salwyn Schapiro, Robinson's former students, produced newer texts in this field.[13]

The accompanying *Readings in Modern European History* also sold extensively, over 26,000 copies of volume one and over 31,000 copies of volume two being sold from 1914 to 1944.[14]

Robinson was reaching hundreds of thousands of students and teachers through his famous college textbooks. Equally significant was his influence, as professor of history at Columbia, upon a group of graduate students who were later to become prominent historians and educators. Some of the more prominent of these were: James T. Shotwell, Charles A. Beard, Carl Becker, William R. Shepherd, Preserved Smith, J. Salwyn Schapiro, Carlton J. H. Hayes, Lynn Thorndike, Alexander C.

---

9. Department of History, Dartmouth College, *Syllabus of Modern History Course 1500-1920,* 1920-21, edition. Part I of this edition which included modern European history 1500-1799, was compiled by Herbert D. Foster, Frank M. Anderson, Charles R. Lingley, Arthur H. Basye, Lewis D. Stilwell, and Leonard C. Jones; Part II, modern European history 1799-1920, by Herbert D. Foster, Frank M. Anderson and Arthur H. Basye.

10. Interview with Schapiro, May 11, 1945; also confirmed by the College of the City of New York *Annual Register 1909-1916;* see appropriate pages.

11. Letter from publisher, August 31, 1944.

12. See pp. 81-3.

13. Carlton, J. H. Hayes, *A Political and Social History of Modern Europe,* 2 vols., New York, Macmillan, 1916, and J. Salwyn Schapiro, *Modern and Contemporary European History,* New York, Houghton Mifflin, 1918.

14. Letter from publisher, August 31, 1944.

Flick, Howard Robinson, Arthur M. Schlesinger, Harold U. Faulkner, Dixon Ryan Fox, Louise R. Loomis, James E. Gillespie, J. Montgomery Gambrill, Edwin P. Tanner, Henry Johnson, David S. Muzzey, Parker T. Moon, Leland Jenks, Martha Arnstein, Mary E. Townsend, Thomas Jesse Jones, Harry J. Carman, Edward Reisner, Max Cushing, Robert L. Schuyler, John Herman Randall Jr., William K. Boyd, and Harry Elmer Barnes.[15] Several of these wrote school or college texts.

Lynn Thorndike, in speaking of Robinson's influence on his graduate students, said: "It seems preferable to remember him as a best teacher and I am inclined to think that his most beneficial and far-reaching intellectual influence was exerted during the first decade of the century when Shotwell, Beard, Hayes, Schapiro, Preserved Smith, David Muzzey, Louise Loomis, Boyd and others were taking courses and writing dissertations under him."[16]

Similarly, Robinson's interest in and enthusiasm for the intellectual phases of man's past were imparted to some of his more prominent students, who later made valuable contributions to this field. Some of the more notable of such contributions were: Carl L. Becker's *The Declaration of Independence: A Study in the History of Political Ideas* and *The Heavenly City of the Eighteenth Century Philosophers*;[17] Dixon Ryan Fox's *Ideas in Motion*;[18] Harry Elmer Barnes' *An Intellectual and Cultural History of the Western World*;[19] Lynn Thorndike's *Science and Thought in the Fifteenth Century: Studies in the History of Medicine and Surgery, Natural and Mathematical Science, Philosophy and Politics*, and *University Records and Life in the Middle Ages*;[20] Carlton J.

---

15. Some names on this list were supplied by Barnes in Odum, *op. cit.*, p. 388; others were supplied during interviews with Robinson's former students, Harry J. Carman, Thomas Jesse Jones, and others.

16. Lynn Thorndike, *op. cit.*, p. 367.

17. Carl Becker, *The Declaration of Independence: A Study in the History of Political Ideas*, New York, Harcourt Brace, 1922, and *The Heavenly City of the Eighteenth Century Philosophers*, New Haven, Yale University Press, 1932.

18. Dixon Ryan Fox, *Ideas in Motion*, New York, Appleton-Century, 1935.

19. Harry Elmer Barnes, *An Intellectual and Cultural History of the Western World*, New York, The Cordon, Co; 1937.

20. Lynn Thorndike, *Science and Thought in the Fifteenth Century: Studies in the History of Medicine and Surgery, Natural and Mathematical Science, Philosophy and Politics*, New York, Columbia University Press, 1929, and *University Records and Life in the Middle Ages*, New York, Columbia University Press, 1944.

H. Hayes' Studies of Nationalism and college texts;[21] John Herman Randall's *The Making of the Modern Mind;*[22] and Preserved Smith's *A History of Modern Culture.*[23]

It was quite natural that those students of Robinson who later became teachers should carry over into their teaching an interest in cultural and intellectual history instilled by Robinson's own enthusiasm. At Columbia David S. Muzzey offered a course entitled The History of European Thought and Culture,[24] Lynn Thorndike still offers one entitled The Intellectual History of Western Europe from the Time of Petrarch to the French Encyclopedia[25] and Carlton J. H. Hayes, through his courses on nationalism,[26] gave much emphasis to the cultural and intellectual aspects of the past. At Cornell Preserved Smith offered a course in The History of Culture from the Renaissance to the Enlightenment.[27] Thus was the focus of attention on the cultural and intellectual aspects of the past continued through both the writing and the teaching done by former students of Robinson. Through them it percolated into many courses taken by teachers and the texts that they use in their classrooms.

Thus far Robinson's more direct influence through his texts and teaching has been indicated. However, this by no means reveals the full extent of his influence. As with any individual who teaches large groups of students and who writes for many readers, Robinson exerted considerable indirect influence, difficult to trace and too elusive to measure.

Dean Harry J. Carman of Columbia College stated that although Robinson was not directly involved he was indirectly one of the inspirers of

21. Carlton J. H. Hayes, *Essays on Nationalism*, New York, Macmillan, 1928, *The Historical Evolution of Modern Nationalism*, New York R. R. Smith Inc., 1932, *France, A Nation of Patriots*, New York, Columbia University Press, 1930, and *A Political and Cultural History of Modern Europe*, 2 vols., New York, Macmillan 1932.
22. John Herman Randall, *The Making of the Modern Mind*, (A Survey of the Intellectual Background of the Present Age), Boston, Houghton Mifflin, 1926.
23. Preserved Smith, *A History of Modern Culture*, 2 vols. New York, Henry Holt, 1930-1934.
24. *Columbia University Catalogue*, 1920-21, p. 153.
25. *Ibid.*, 1928-29, p. 220.
26. *Ibid.*
27. Cornell University *Official Bulletin*, XXIII, 1932-33, p. 60.

the course in Contemporary Civilization first offered at Columbia in 1919.[28] This course which aimed "(1) to inform the student of the most outstanding and influential factors of his physical and social environment; (2) to survey the historical background of contemporary civilization; (3) to raise for consideration the insistent problems of the present; (4) to enable the student to understand the civilization of his own day and to participate more effectively in it; and (5) finally to give the student early in his college course objective material on which to base his own further studies," certainly fulfilled Robinson's requirements for the "new history."[29]

Dr. Schapiro gave another example of Robinson's indirect influence on teaching of college history. Dr. Schapiro, in an interview with the writer, stated that Robinson directly inspired him to initiate in 1916 the first course in intellectual history at the College of the City of New York. This course, entitled Intellectual History of Europe during the Nineteenth Century, met with such success that the following year another course in this field was added, Intellectual History of Europe Since the French Revolution. In these courses hundreds of students were brought into contact with many of Robinson's concepts of intellectual history. Among Dr. Schapiro's students was Herbert M. Morais, who became so interested in the possibilities of intellectual history that when he later became an instructor at Brooklyn College he initiated in that institution the first courses in this phase of European history.[30]

In addition to teaching many graduate students who later gained prominence as historians, Robinson exerted an immeasurable influence on the thousands of elementary and high school teachers from Teachers College who attended his popular course, The History of the Intellectual Class in Western Europe. Henry Johnson, Professor Emeritus of History at Teachers College, states that "practically everyone" at Teachers College had a course with Robinson during Robinson's last few years at Columbia.[31] This is confirmed by another of his former

---

28. Interview with Dean Harry J. Carman, May 22, 1945. William R. Shepherd, James T. Shotwell, Robert L. Schuyler and Dixon Ryan Fox were among others to whom the course owned part of its inspiration.
29. Harry J. Carman, "The Columbia Course in Contemporary Civilization," Association of History Teachers of the Middle States and Maryland, *Proceedings*, 1925, p. 41.
30. Interview with J. Salwyn Schapiro, May 11, 1945. This was also confirmed by the *Brooklyn College Bulletin*, 1932-33, p. 83.
31. Interview with Henry Johnson, June 3, 1945.

students, Dr. Irwin Edman, who, in speaking of the size and composition of Robinson's classes, said, "The majority of the class of over 200 were graduate students of history many of them women high school teachers from all over the country, particularly the West and South.[32]

As has already been indicated, this study of the intellectual history of western Europe was not a traditional course in political, economic, or military history; rather it was an attempt to utilize history to show the need for bringing the human mind up to date. Robinson, in this class, was especially critical both of man's natural reverence for the familiar, for the habitual, and also for his reluctance to break from the past. This habit of man, he pointed out, was especially unfortunate in view of the fact that man now had at his command the available knowledge, ingenuity, and natural resources to make a far fairer world than that in which he now found himself. Robinson suggested, however, that before man could fully capitalize on his new position, he must change the traditional pattern of thought and action which had been handed down to him by earlier generations who had lived under very different conditions and who had possessed far less information about the world and themselves.

Robinson argued that the study of history revealed that the fundamental product of human experience was progress and that institutions and ideas were not the product of human nature but of human nurture, as he was fond of calling it. History as he saw it and taught it was not a supporter of the argument of the conservatives for maintaining the *status quo* but rather was a weapon to be seized by the radical and used in behalf of social betterment. In speaking of the possibility of utilizing history as a weapon for reform, Robinson said, "History would seem to discredit conservatism as a working principle in view of the vast achievements of mankind in the recent past and of the possibilities which open before us."[33] This was the liberal philosophy of history which Robinson imparted directly to hundreds of elementary and secondary school teachers who attended his classes each year, and indirectly to hundreds more in the classrooms of his former students.

In addition to Robinson's influence as a classroom teacher, he exerted a wide influence on the teaching of history in the secondary schools in

32. Irwin Edman, *Philosopher's Holiday*, p. 119.
33. Robinson, *Outline of the History of the Intellectual Class in Western Europe*, New York, Marcon Press, 1914, pp. 53-56.

other ways: namely, as author and co-author of history textbooks on the secondary level, and as an active member of professional organizations and committees considering the place of history in the secondary school.

As an author and co-author of history textbooks for the secondary field Robinson's prestige was great. Figures for only two of his high school texts reveal sales for over a million copies: *The History of Western Europe: Ancient and Medieval*,[34] written in collaboration with James Henry Breasted, totaled over 850,000 copies; *Our World Today and Yesterday*, written with the collaboration of Breasted and Emma Peters Smith, sold over 290,000 copies.[35] Unfortunately sales figures are unavailable on his most popular texts, *Medieval and Modern Times* and the *History of Europe: Our Own Times*, done in collaboration with Beard; but both texts went through several editions.

As has already been shown, Robinson in writing his secondary-school texts drew heavily from the material appearing in two of his earlier college texts,[36] *An Introduction to the History of Western Europe* (written 1902-3) and the *Development of Modern Europe* (written 1907-8 and produced in collaboration with Beard). In some cases Robinson's high school texts were little more than college texts with a discussion of the cultural, intellectual, and economic phases of the past omitted or greatly reduced.[37] Robinson's practice of utilizing the material appearing in his earlier college texts and his reluctance to include in his high school texts more material on the cultural, economic, and intellectual phases of the past (the inclusion of which was an innovation which had given fame to his *Introduction to the History of Western Europe*), caused his secondary-school texts to appear quite traditional by 1921. This does not mean that his secondary texts were similar to the texts of 1900; rather his textbooks were taking a middle ground more in line with the trends of the times than were the more traditional texts of Myers,[38] yet by no means approaching Webster[39] in a generous treatment of the cultural, economic, and intellectual aspects

---

34. This was taken from Part I of the *Outlines of European History*, published by the same authors in 1914.
35. Letter from publisher, August 31, 1944.
36. See page 94 (Chapter 3).
37. See page 91 (Chapter 3).
38. Myers, *Medieval and Modern History* (1919), see above, p. 96.
39. Webster, Medieval and Modern History (1919), see pp. 96-9.
of this work.

of the past. However, it appears that Robinson's first secondary-school text, *Outlines of European History* (published in 1912 and 1916), done in collaboration with Beard and Breasted, was influential in leading the swing to world history in the secondary-school.[40]

Although Robinson's secondary-school texts were on the whole less venturesome and more traditional than his earlier college texts, he continued to have a liberalizing influence on the teaching of history in the secondary schools through his activities in professional organizations and his membership on professional committees considering the place of history in the secondary-schools. The Association of the Colleges and Preparatory Schools of the Middle States and Maryland, the American Historical Association, the New England History Teachers' Association, the National Herbart Society, the Association of History Teachers of the Middle States and Maryland, and the National Education Association heard Robinson's plea for the teaching of a new type of history which would more nearly fill the educational and social requirements of our modern age.[41]

The extent to which these ideas were accepted by historians and teachers was revealed by the support given to his recommendations in the 1904 meeting of the Association of History Teachers of the Middle States and Maryland,[42] and in the Report of the Committee of Five of the American Historical Association.[43]

Probably the most important was his influence exerted through the Report of the Committee on the Social Studies published in 1916. This report embodying many of the ideas appearing in Robinson's *New History*, was widely circulated by the United States Bureau of Education and exerted a great influence on the social studies curriculum of the secondary-schools.[44]

As has been shown, Robinson as a classroom teacher, as an author of history textbooks, and as a champion and popularizer of the "new history" exerted a tremendous influence on the teaching of European history in colleges and in secondary schools. The extent to which Robinson's earlier ideas had become a part of the dominant philosophy

40. See chapter 3, p. 92; also see Wayland J. Chase, "Review of Robinson and Breasted—Outlines of European History," *The History Teachers' Magazine*, vol. VI, October, 1915, p. 266.
41. See above pp. 47-50.
42. See above pp. 54-7.
43. See above pp. 58, 59.
44. See above pp. 63-4.

of history and the social studies by the third decade of the present century may be grasped by examining authentic statements of that time concerning the nature and function of history and its social science allies. Probably the most important statements of this nature are contained in the significant report of the Commission on the Social Studies appointed in 1929 by the American Historical Association.[45] Two volumes of this report, *A Charter for the Social Sciences* and *The Nature of the Social Sciences*,[46] both written by Charles A. Beard at the request of the commission, are especially significant inasmuch as they were subjected to the suggestions and criticisms of the entire commission and therefore represented to a large degree the composite ideas of the commission.[47] A comparison of some of the major concepts of history expressed in these two volumes, by Beard and the members of the commission, with those expressed earlier by Robinson will reveal the degree to which his earlier concepts had come to be accepted by historians and educators.

The commission accepted Robinson's earlier ideas as to the comprehensiveness of history, the privilege of the historian to select facts from the past to suit the particular needs of the time, the desirability of selecting those from the past which would throw light on present-day problems, the interdependence of history and its social science allies, and the value of history in demonstrating the inevitability of change.

Robinson, in writing of the comprehensiveness of history, in 1912, had said, "In its amplest meaning History includes every trace of everything that man has ever done or thought since he first appeared on the earth."[48] Beard, in *The Nature of the Social Sciences,* agreed that history covered the whole reach of time from the "dateless beginning to the latest hours."[49]

Also the commission acknowledged the privilege of the historian

---

45. This Commission conducted an exhaustive investigation. The results were published in sixteen volumes which appeared at intervals between 1932 and 1936. Some of the most important men on this Commission, Charles A. Beard, Henry Johnson, Guy Stanton Ford, and Carlton, J. H. Hayes, were former students of Robinson.
46. Charles A. Beard, *A Charter for the Social Sciences*, (Report of the Commission on the Social Studies, Part I) Scribners, 1932. Charles A. Beard, *The Nature of the Social Sciences*, (Report of the Commission on The Social Sciences), Scribner, 1934.
47. Beard, *Charter*, Preface. Also *The Nature of Social Sciences*, Preface.
48. Robinson, *New History*, p. 1.
49. Beard, *The Nature of the Social Sciences*, p. 50.

to select and arrange the material from the past to suit the purpose at hand. As in *The Nature of the Social Sciences:* "All facts are not included in any history; those which are included do not select themselves. They are chosen and ordered by the historian with reference to some of ideas, purposes, and philosophy which he has in mind, more or less consciously."[50] Robinson in his *New History* had stated it thus: "Each age has a perfect right to select from the annals of mankind those facts that seem to have a particular bearing on the matters it has at heart."[51]

In a similar manner the commission expressed its agreement with two other important ideas appearing in Robinson's *New History:* namely, that history might well make its most useful contribution to the study of man by explaining the origin of many of our contemporary problems,[52] and that the historian in applying himself to this task should look upon the other social sciences as allies. Robinson, in 1912, had called the attention of his fellow historians to the fact that the bounds of all departments of human knowledge were inherently provisional, indefinite, and fluctuating, and that history to secure its maximum development and to render its greatest service must be willing to surrender its individualistic aspirations and to recognize that it was but one of the many ways of studying mankind.[53] Two decades later, the commission, in the *Charter of the Social Sciences,* acknowledged that during the past fifteen years there had been a "marked tendency to cut across the conventional subject matter boundaries in every direction."[54]

The commission was equally in accord with Robinson's observations on the changing nature of our modern age. Robinson, in his *Mind in the Making,* recognizing the challenge being offered by the discovery of vast amounts of new knowledge, observed that nothing was going to be settled in the same sense as things were once supposed to be settled, the simple reason being that knowledge would probably continue to increase and would inevitably alter the world, with which man would have to make terms.[55] In the *Charter of the Social Sciences* Beard, too, acknowledged the changing nature of our world: "After the

50. Beard, *op. cit.,* pp. 50-51.
51. Robinson, *op. cit.,* p. 135.
52. *Ibid.,* p. 17. Beard, *Nature of the Social Sciences,* pp. 50-53.
53. Robinson, *op. cit.,* pp. 73-74.
54. Beard, *Charter of the Social Sciences,* pp. 20-21.
55. Robinson, *Mind in the Making,* p. 212.

assembled wisdom has said its last word, the still small voice of discovery will be heard in unexpected and unofficial quarters, and new planets will swing into the ken of watchers."[56]

Such a probability, Beard felt, had important educational implications; for in our world, where fundamental changes were taking place, there was a very real danger in overemphasizing the importance of the traditional or conventional. That this might be avoided, Beard urged the need for developing attitudes and aptitudes appropriate to a rapidly developing world.[57] This recommendation of Beard and that of the commission echoed Robinson, who two decades earlier had warned against the danger of giving "precedents a perpetual value" and observed that all too often man's respect for a given institution or social convention was purely traditional and had little relation to its value as judged by evisting conditions.[58]

Thus it would seem that the American Historical Association through its Commission on the Social Studies had come to accept the basic concepts of the "new history": namely, the comprehensiveness of history, the necessity for its close cooperation with the other social science allies, its obligation to select those facts from the past that would aid in the solution of contemporary problems, and lastly by explanation of the origins of many traditions and beliefs, history's capacity to free our minds so that we might be prepared to make necessary adjustments to our rapidly changing world.

56. Beard, *Charter*, p. 1.
57. *Ibid.*, p. 113.
58. Robinson, *New History*, p. 22.

Bibliography

The most important sources available for this study have been the addresses and writings of Robinson himself. Many of these are scattered through professional periodicals such as the *American Historical Review,* the *Political Science Quarterly, Journal of Philosophy, Psychology and the Scientific Method,* the *Annals of the American Academy of Political and Social Science,* the *International Monthly,* and the *Educational Bi-Monthly,* and the proceedings, minutes and annual reports of various professional organizations such as the Association of Colleges and Preparatory Schools of the Middle States and Maryland, the American Historical Association, the Association of History Teachers of the Middle States and Maryland, the National Herbart Society and the New England History Teachers' Association. Equally important were three other major sources, the *New History,* the college and secondary school texts of which Robinson was author or co-author, and the official reports of professional committees concerned with the place of history in the schools, such as: "Report of the Sub-committee on History, Civil Government, and Political Economy of the Committee on the Secondary School Studies of the National Educational Association," "Report of the Special Committee on College Entrance Requirements of the Association of History Teachers of the Middle States and Maryland," "Report of the Committee of Five of the American Historical Association" and lastly the "Report of the Committee on the Social Studies of the Commission on the Reorganization of Secondary Education." Unfortunately there exist no notes or records of the deliberations of these committees.

The Robinson papers which have been of limited value in this investigation are in possession of Clifton H. Bushnell, Robinson's nephew and one time secretary. They include various editions of Robinson's books, Robinson's collection of rare books, hundreds of newspaper clippings, containing book reviews, a number of letters from various sections of the United States, Europe and the Orient commenting upon Robinson's *Mind in the Making* and the *Humanizing of Knowledge,* and some correspondence of Robinson's during his later years (after 1918). The collection includes no correspondence for the early period of Robinson's career. The most valuable correspondence was a series of weekly letters that Robinson had written to his sister, Sarah. Although they dealt generally with personal and family affairs they frequently gave interesting insights into Robinson's ideas and plans.

Another valuable source for this study has been the writer's interviews with some of Robinson's former students and associates. They are: Henry Johnson, professor emeritus of history of Teachers College; Harry J. Carman, now dean of Columbia College; Virginia Gildersleeve, dean of Barnard College; James T. Shotwell, professor emeritus of history of Columbia and now with the Carnegie Endowment for International Peace; J. Salwyn Schapiro; professor of history in the College of the City of New York; Thomas Jesse Jones, director of the Philip Stokes Foundation; Alvin Johnson, former president of the New School for Social Research; and Wesley Mitchell, professor emeritus of economics of Columbia and former associate with Robinson at the New School for Social Research.

ROBINSON'S PUBLICATIONS

College Textbooks and Syllabi

The Development of Modern Europe; An Introduction to the Study of Current History. (With Charles Austin Beard.) Boston, Ginn and Company, 1907-1908, 2 vols. [Completely revised and enlarged edition, 1929-1930, 2 vols.]

An Introduction to the History of Western Europe, Boston, Ginn and Company, 1902-1903, 2 vols. [Completely revised and enlarged edition, 1924-1926, and in 1934; Chinese translation of vol. I, 1924-25, Urdu translation 1929.]

The Last Decade of European History and the Great War; designed as a supplement to the *Development of Modern History* and an *Introduction to the History of Western Europe,* Boston, Ginn and Company, 1918, pp. 74. [After 1918 this was bound with *An Introduction to the History of Western Europe.*]

Outline of the History of the Intellectual Class of Western Europe, New York, Privately printed, 1911, pp. 58.

Outline of the History of the Intellectual Class of Western Europe. New York, Marion Press, 1914, pp. 56.

Source Material (Books)

Petrarch, The First Modern Scholar and Man of Letters; A Selection from His Correspondence with Boccaccio and Other Friends, Designed To Illustrate the Beginnings of the Renaissance. Translated with Henry Winchester Rolfe, New York, G. P. Putnam's Sons, 1898, x, pp. 436.

Readings in European History; A Collection of Extracts from the Sources Chosen with the Purpose of Illustrating the Progress of Culture in Western Europe Since the German Invasions. Boston, Ginn and Company, 1904-1906, 2 vols.

Readings in Modern European History; A Collection of Extracts from the Sources Chosen with the Purpose of Illustrating Some of the Chief Phases of the Development of Europe During the Last Two Hundred Years. (With Charles Austin Beard), Boston, Ginn and Company, 1908-1909, 2 vols.

Some source material appearing in the series of *Translations and Reprints* published by the Department of History at the University of Pennsylvania.

The French Revolution, 1789-1791. Philadelphia, 1894, pp. 32. (University of Pennsylvania, Department of History, Translations and Reprints, vol. I, No. 5.)

The Napoleonic Period. Philadelphia, 1895, pp. 32. (University of Pennsylvania, Depart. of History, Translations and Reprints, vol. II, No. 2.)

The Period of Early Reformation in Germany. Philadelphia, 1895, pp. 32. (University of Pennsylvania, Department of History, Translations and Reprints, vol. II, No. 6.)

The Restoration and the European Policy of Metternich, 1814-1820. Philadelphia, 1896, pp. 24. (University of Pennsylvania, Department of History, Translations and Reprints, vol. I, No. 3.)

The Pre-Reformation Period. Philadelphia, 1897, pp. 34. (University of Pennsylvania, Department of History, Translations and Reprints, vol. III, No. 6.)

Protest of The Cour Des Aides of Paris, 10 April 1775. Editor. Philadelphia, 1899, viii, pp. 154. (University of Pennsylvania, Department of History, Translations and Reprints, vol. V, No. 2.)

Secondary School Textbooks

A General History of Europe, from the Origins of Civilization to the Present Time (with James Henry Breasted and Emma Peters Smith). Boston, Ginn and Company, 1921, xiv, pp. 667.

History of Europe; Our Own Times, The Eighteenth and Nineteenth Centuries: The Opening of the Twentieth Century and the World War (with Charles Austin Beard). Boston, Ginn and Company, 1921, xii, pp. 616. (Revised editions, 1927 xii, pp. 654; 1934, xii, pp. 658.)

Medieval and Modern Times; An Introduction to the History of Europe from the Dissolution of the Roman Empire to the Opening of the Great War of 1914. Boston, Ginn and Company, 1916, xii, pp. 777.

Our World Today and Yesterday (with James Henry Breasted and Emma Peters Smith), Boston, Ginn and Company, 1924, xiv, pp. 625. This is largely based upon the authors' earlier text *A General History of Europe,* 1921.

Outlines of European History (with James Henry Breasted and Charles Austin Beard), Boston, Ginn and Company, 1912-14, 2 vols.

Other Books

The Human Comedy, New York, Harper, 1937, xvii, pp. 394. (Selections from Robinson's earlier writings prepared and edited by Harry Elmer Barnes.)

The Humanizing of Knowledge, New York, George H. Doran Company, 1923, ix, pp. 117.

The Mind in the Making; The Relation of Intelligence to Social Reform,
New York, Harper and Brothers, 1921, pp. 235.
The New History; Essays Illustrating the Modern Historical Outlook,
New York, The Macmillan Company, 1911, vii, pp. 266.
The Ordeal of Civilization; A Sketch of the Development and World-Wide Diffusion of Our Present Day Institutions and Ideas. New York, Harper and Brothers, 1926, xii, pp. 769. (Reprinted in large part from *Medieval and Modern Times.*)

Addresses and Articles

"Sidgwick's Elements of Politics," *Annals of the American Academy of Political and Social Science,* September, 1892, vol. III, pp. 211-222.

"Ought the Sources To Be Used in Teaching History?" *Proceedings* of the Second Annual Convention of the Association of Colleges and Preparatory Schools in the Middle States and Maryland, 1894, pp. 38-44.

"Tennis Court Oath," *Annual Report of the American Historical Association,* 1894, pp. 541-547.

"The Teaching of European History in the College" *Annual Report of the American Historical Association,* 1896, vol. I, pp. 265-278.

"Teaching of History in the Secondary Schools" *Proceedings* of the Twelfth Annual Convention of the Association of Colleges and Preparatory Schools of the Middle States and Maryland, 1898, pp. 8-12.

"The French Declaration of the Rights of Man of 1789," *Political Science Quarterly,* December 1899, vol. XIV, pp. 653-662.

"Medieval History in the High School," *National Herbart Society, Fifth Yearbook,* 1899, pp. 42-68.

"Sacred and Profane History," *Annual Report of the American Historical Association,* 1899, vol. I, pp. 527-535.

"Popular Histories: Their Defects and Possibilities," *International Monthly,* July 1900, vol. II, pp. 47-73.

"The Neglect of the Church by Historians," *Political Science Quarterly,* December 1900, vol. XV, pp. 667-674.

"The Study of the Lutheran Revolt," *American Historical Review,* January, 1903, vol. VIII, pp. 205-216.

"The Conception and Methods of History." (In Howard J. Rogers (editor) *Congress of Arts and Science, Universal Exposition, St. Louis, 1904,* Boston, Houghton Mifflin, 1906, pp. 658) pp. 40-51.

"Recent Tendencies in the Study of the French Revolution," *American Historical Review,* April, 1906, vol. XI, pp. 529-547.

The Fall of Rome: Some Current Misapprehensions in Regard to the Process of Dissolution of the Roman Empire, Boston, New England History Teachers' Association, 1907, pp. 27. (Published as a pamphlet.) Revised and reprinted in the *New History,* 1912.

History, New York, Columbia University Press, 1908, pp. 25. Revised and reprinted in the *New History,* 1912.

"How To Make History More Definite," *Minutes* of the Seventh Annual

Convention of the Association of History Teachers of the Middle States and Maryland, 1909, pp. 6-11.

"The Significance of History in Industrial Education," *Educational Bi-Monthly,* June 1910, vol. IV, pp. 376-389.

"The Spirit of Conservatism in the Light of History," *Journal of Philosophy, Psychology, and Scientific Methods,* May 1911, vol. VIII, pp. 253-269. Revised and reprinted in the *New History,* 1912.

"Relation of History to the Newer Sciences of Man," *Journal of Philosophy, Psychology and the Scientific Method,* vol. VIII, 1911, pp. 141-157. Revised and printed in the *New History,* 1911.

"The New School," *School and Society,* January 1920, vol. XI, pp. 129-132.

"Civilization," *Encyclopaedia Britannica,* Fourteenth edition, New York, 1929, vol. V, pp. 735-741.

CONTEMPORARY TEXTBOOKS USED FOR COMPARISON

College Textbooks

Adams, George B., *Medieval and Modern History: An Outline of Its Development,* New York, The Macmillan Company, 1901, ix, pp. 474.

Andrews, Charles M., *The Historical Development of Modern Europe from the Congress of Vienna to the Present Times.* New York, G. P. Putnam's Sons, 1896, 2 vols.

Fyffe, Charles A., *A History of Modern Europe, 1792-1878,* New York, Henry Holt, 1896, xi, pp. 1088.

Myers, Philip Van Ness, *Medieval and Modern History,* Boston, Ginn and Company, 1902-1903, 2 vols.

Seignobos, Charles, *A Political History of Europe Since 1814;* translated by Charles M. MacLane. New York, Henry Holt, 1899, xxi, pp. 881.

Stephens, H. Morse, *Syllabus of a Course of Eighty-Seven Lectures on Modern European History.* New York, The Macmillan Company, 1899, ix, pp. 319.

Secondary School Textbooks

Becker, Carl I., *Modern History,* New York, Silver, Burdett and Company, 1933, viii, pp. 825.

Elson, Henry W., *Modern Times and the Living Past,* New York, D. C. Heath, 1921, iv, pp. 728.

Myers, Philip Van Ness, *Medieval and Modern History,* Boston, Ginn and Company, 1920, xiv, pp. 672.

Webster, Hutton, *Medieval and Modern History,* New York, D. C. Heath, 1919, iv, pp. 787.

Webster, Hutton, *Modern European Civilization,* New York, D. C. Heath, 1933, vi, pp. 795.

Webster, Hutton, *World History*, New York, D. C. Heath, 1921, iv, pp. 759.

West, Willis M., *The Story of World Progress*, New York, Allyn and Bacon, 1922, xix, pp. 669.

GENERAL REFERENCES

Committee Reports

Report of the Committee of Ten on Secondary School Studies. New York, American Book Company, 1894, ii, pp. 162-203.

The Study of History in Schools: Report to the American Historical Association by the Committee of Seven. New York, The Macmillan Company, 1899, vi, pp. 267.

"Report of the Committee on College Entrance Requirements in History," *Minutes* of the Second Annual Convention of the Association of History Teachers of the Middle States and Maryland, 1904, pp. 30-38, for discussion of the report, pp. 41-51.

The Study of History in Secondary Schools: Report to the American Historical Association by the Committee of Five. New York, The Macmillan Company, 1911, pp. 74.

The Social Studies in Secondary Education: Report of the Committee on the Social Studies of the Commission on the Reorganization of Secondary Education, United States Bureau of Education, Bulletin, 1916, Number 28, pp. 63.

Books

Adams, Herbert B. and others, *Methods in Teaching History,* Boston, D. C. Heath and Company, 1889, xiv, pp. 391.

Adams, Herbert B., *The Study of History in American Colleges and Universities,* Bureau of Education Circular of Information Number 2, Washington, Government Printing Office, 1887, pp. 299.

Barnes, Harry Elmer, "James Harvey Robinson" (In Odum, Howard W., *American Masters of Social Science,* New York, Henry Holt and Company, 1927, vi, pp. 411), pp. 321-408.

Barnes, Mary Sheldon, *Studies in Historical Method,* Boston, D. C. Heath and Company, 1896, iv, pp. 114.

Beard, Charles A., *A Charter for the Social Sciences* (Report of the Commission on the Social Studies Part I), New York, Charles Scribner's Sons, 1932, xii, pp. 117.

Beard, Charles A., *The Nature of the Social Sciences* (Report of the Commission on the Social Studies, Part VII), New York, Charles Scribner's Sons, 1934, x, pp. 236.

Cheyney, Edward P., *History of the University of Pennsylvania,* Philadelphia, University of Pennsylvania Press, 1940, x, pp. 461.

Edman, Irwin, *Philosopher's Holiday,* New York, Viking Press, 1938, x, pp. 270.

Hayes, Carlton J. H., *A Political and Social History of Europe,* New York, The Macmillan Company, 1916, 2 vols.

Johnson, Henry, *The Other Side of Main Street,* New York, Columbia University Press, 1943, viii, pp. 263.

Johnson, Henry, *Teaching of History in Elementary and Secondary Schools,* New York, The Macmillan Company, 1915, xviii, pp. 497.

Johnson, Henry, *Teaching of History in Elementary and Secondary Schools with Applications to Allied Studies,* New York, The Macmillan Company, 1940, xv, pp. 467.

Miller, Alice D., *Barnard College: The First Fifty Years,* New York, Columbia University Press, 1939, xiii, pp. 194.

Salmon, Lucy M., "Some Principles in the Teaching of History," *First Yearbook* of the National Society for the Scientific Study of Education, Part I, Chicago, University of Chicago Press, 1902, pp. 74.

Schapiro, J. Salwyn, *Modern and Contemporary European History,* Boston, Houghton Mifflin Company, 1918, xi, pp. 840.

Trenholme, Norman M., *A Syllabus for the History of Western Europe,* Boston, Ginn and Company, 1907, 2 vols.

Tryon, Rolla M., *The Social Studies as School Subjects* (Report of the Commission on the Social Studies, Part XI), New York, Scribner's Sons, 1935, xiii, pp. 541.

Tryon, Rolla M., *The Teaching of History in the Junior and Senior High School,* New York, Ginn and Company, 1921, iv, pp. 294.

Wesley, Edgar, *Teaching the Social Studies,* New York, D. C. Heath and Company, 1937, xvii, pp. 635.

Articles and Addresses

Carman, Harry J., "The Columbia Course in Contemporary Civilization," Association of History Teachers of the Middle States and Maryland, *Proceedings,* 1925, pp. 40-47.

Davenport, F. G., "Readings in European History" (Review), *American Historical Review,* vol. XXII, October, 1906, pp. 168-169.

Fay, Sidney B., "The Development of Modern Europe: An Introduction to the Study of Current History" (Review), *American Historical Review,* vol. XIV, October, 1909, pp. 188-190.

Fay, Sidney B., "Robinson and Beard's Development of Modern Europe" (Review), *History Teachers' Magazine,* vol. I, 1909, pp. 35.

The Nation, "An Introduction to the History of Western Europe" (Review), vol. LXXVI, June 18, 1903, pp. 502-3 (unsigned review).

Packard, Sidney R., "The Introductory College Course in History," *Social Education,* vol. IV, December, 1940, pp. 538-544.

Robinson, Edward Van Dyke, "Medieval and Modern History in the High Schools," *School Review,* vol. VIII, May 1909, pp. 268-270.

Schapiro, J. Salwyn, "James Harvey Robinson 1863-1936," *Journal of Social Philosophy,* vol. I, April, '936, pp. 278-281.

Sellery, George C., "An Introduction to the History of Western Europe"

(Review), *Annals of the American Academy of Political and Social Science,* vol. XXIII, January, 1904, pp. 165-6.

Shortridge, W. P., "Robinson and Beard's Outlines of European History" (Review), *History Teachers' Magazine,* vol. IV, November 1913, pp. 269-270.

Strayer, Joseph R., "What Is Medieval History?" *Social Education,* vol. IX, November 1945, pp. 293-294.

Thorndike, Lynn, "A Review of the Human Comedy by James Harvey Robinson (1937)," *Journal of Modern History,* vol. IX, September, 1937, pp. 36-41.

Newspapers and Periodicals

The American Hebrew, New York City, June 19, 1903.

Bloomington *Bulletin,* Bloomington, Illinois, April 30, 1911.

Bloomington *Pantagraph,* Bloomington, Illinois. (Many undated clippings in the Bushnell Collection.)

Catholic Mirror, Baltimore, Maryland, November 26, 1904.

State Journal, Columbus, Ohio, June 14, 1903.

Miscellaneous

"Bibliography of James Harvey Robinson" (Reprint from a Bibliography of the Faculty of Political Science, Columbia University 1830-1931), Columbia University Press, 1931.

Brooklyn College, *Bulletin,* 1932-1933.

College of the City of New York, *Annual Register,* 1909-1916.

Columbia College *Catalogue,* 1893-1896.

Columbia University in the City of New York, *Catalogue,* 1897-1920.

Columbia University in the City of New York, *Seventh Annual Report* of President Low to the Trustees, 1896.

Cornell University, *Official Bulletin,* vol. XXIII, 1932-1933.

Department of History, Dartmouth College, *Syllabus of Modern History Course 1500-1920,* 1921.

New School for Social Research, *Announcement 1920-26.*

University of Pennsylvania, *Catalogue of Announcements,* 1891-1894.